You're still poor because no one ever showed you how money really works. You were told to work harder, save what you can, and hope it adds up. That advice doesn't work.

The truth is you're poor because of the habits you keep, the myths you believe, and the actions you avoid. More money won't fix it. A raise won't fix it. A lottery ticket won't fix it. Only a new plan will.

This book is that plan. Straightforward. Practical. Built for the real world. Read it, apply it, and your financial life will change. Ignore it, and nothing will.

—Alexis Buchholz
Managing Partner, BFG Wealth Management

Why You're Still Poor

Why You're Still Poor

And What To Do About It

Alexis Buchholz

BFG WEALTH
MANAGEMENT

BFG Wealth Management
3838 Oak Lawn Ave Ste 1000
Dallas, TX 75219

Email: info@bfgwm.com
Website: www.bfgwm.com

Published by BFG Wealth Publishing
In association with BFG Wealth Management

Library of Congress Control Number: 2025927720

This book is intended for informational and educational purposes only and does not constitute legal, tax, or financial advice. The author and publisher make no guarantees regarding outcomes or results. Readers should consult qualified professionals before acting on any information contained herein.

Statistics, examples, and references reflect information available at the time of writing. Economic conditions, market performance, inflation levels, tax laws, and regulatory environments change over time.

BFG Wealth Management is a Registered Investment Advisor. Registration with the SEC or any state securities authority does not imply a certain level of skill or training.

Printed in the United States of America
ISBN: 979-8-9943165-0-4 (Paperback)
ISBN: 979-8-9943165-1-1 (Hardcover)
ISBN: 979-8-9943165-2-8 (Ebook)

First Edition

Cover and interior design by Shahla Buchholz

Acknowledgments

To the clients who placed their trust in me: Thank you for allowing me to walk with you through your financial journeys. Your progress, discipline, and resilience showed me that real wealth is built step by step. Your stories shaped the lessons in this book more than any textbook ever could.

To those who hesitated or struggled to act: I am grateful to you as well. Your experiences revealed how powerful the barriers of fear, procrastination, and misinformation can be. You taught me that financial success is not just about numbers, but about behavior, mindset, and systems.

And to you, the reader: Thank you for investing your time here. My hope is that these pages give you both the clarity and the conviction to act. If you take even one principle and apply it consistently, you will be ahead of most. Knowledge is the seed. Action is the harvest.

Contents

Introduction: The Hard Truth About Why You're Still Poor.................... 1

PART I – Why You're Still Poor 7
1. The Money Myths You Believe...10
2. Lifestyle Creep: Spending More Than You Earn..........................21
3. Bad Debt and Credit Addiction...29
4. No Plan, No Progress 41
5. The Hidden Costs of Ignorance 51

PART II – What To Do About It 63
6. The Wealth Mindset Shift 67
7. Cash Flow is King 81
8. Kill the Bad Debt, Build Good Credit..95
9. Investing That Actually Works..117
10. Build Multiple Streams of Income 133
11. Taxes, Protection, and Smart Structures...................................145

Part III – Mastery and Freedom 165
12. Systems Beat Willpower 169
13. Relationships, Networks, and Who You Listen To 183
14. Teaching Wealth to the Next Generation...................................203
15. Your 20-Year Wealth Blueprint...215
Conclusion: Why You're Still Poor - And What to Do About It............229

Sources & References...234
Quick Reference Wealth Terms 236
Appendix: Glossary of Key Terms..240
The Wealth Toolkit..250
Further Reading & Recommended Resources................................252
About the Author..254
Disclosures 255

Introduction: The Hard Truth About Why You're Still Poor

You work. You earn. You grind through weeks, months, and years. Yet your bank account barely moves. The money disappears as fast as it comes in. The debt keeps growing. Financial freedom feels out of reach.

You tell yourself it'll get better when you make more. You tell yourself you just need the right break, a little luck, or a well-deserved raise. But here's the truth. If you're still poor, it's not because of luck. It's not because you were born into the wrong family. It's not even because you don't make enough. You're still poor because of how you handle money, what you believe about it, and the habits you repeat every single day.

Most people never face this. They blame the system, their boss, the economy. Some excuses are real, but excuses don't change anything. What changes everything is taking control of what you *can* control. That starts here.

This book isn't here to comfort you. It's not another "just think positive" pep talk. You don't need sugarcoating. You need a mirror and a blueprint. I'm going to show you the mistakes that keep you poor, and then I'm going to show you the steps to break free. It'll sting at times, but that sting is the beginning of change.

Why Most People Stay Poor
We live in the wealthiest country in history. Information is free. Opportunity is everywhere. Yet millions of people are drowning in debt and living paycheck to paycheck. It's not because there isn't enough money. It's because most people never learn how money actually works.

Schools don't teach it. Parents pass down bad habits. Social media sells fake wealth and get-rich-quick schemes. You end up copying the wrong examples and making the same mistakes. You buy things you don't need, chase trends that don't matter, and call it normal. But being poor isn't normal. It's a trap.

The trap looks different for everyone, but the outcome is the same. Stress. Anxiety. No savings. Always waiting for the next paycheck. Always behind.

Kevin's Story

Kevin makes over a quarter million dollars a year. On paper, he should be rich. In reality, he's poor. He drives luxury cars. He lives in a big house. He travels the world. To everyone else, he looks successful. But behind the curtain, the picture is different.

He has car loans, he has a mortgage that eats up most of his paycheck, and he has credit cards he never pays off. He spends more than he makes. Every dollar is already spoken for before it arrives. If he lost his job tomorrow, he would collapse financially in weeks.

Kevin proves a point most people refuse to believe. More money doesn't fix bad money habits. If you can't manage the smaller amount, you won't magically manage the bigger amount. Without discipline, more income just means bigger mistakes.

Kevin looks like an outlier, but he isn't. There are thousands of Kevins at every income level. Maybe you're one of them.

What This Book Will Do

This book isn't about theory. It's about action, and it's broken into three parts:

- **Part I: Why You're Still Poor.** The myths, lies, and mistakes that drain your money. You will see yourself in these chapters. It may be painful at times, but that's where change begins.

- **Part II: What To Do About It.** The tools that actually build wealth. Budgeting, killing debt, investing the right way, creating income streams, and protecting what you earn.

- **Part III: Mastery and Freedom.** Wealth isn't a finish line. It's a system. You'll learn how to keep your money, avoid the old traps, and build a legacy for your family.

By the time you finish, you'll know exactly why you're stuck financially and exactly how to break free.

The Promise
This isn't instant. It's not easy. If you're looking for a lottery ticket, close this book now. But if you're ready to shift your mindset, take real steps, and stay consistent, this book gives you the plan.

The process is simple, but most people won't do it. They'll keep living like Kevin, spending every dollar and calling it normal. They'll keep swiping the credit card, chasing the next thing, and hoping for a miracle.

You're different. Otherwise, you wouldn't be reading this.

A Challenge to You
Don't just read this book. Use it. Take the steps. Follow the plan. If you do, a year from now your financial life will look completely different.

If you skim it, nod your head, and go back to your old habits, nothing will change. You will stay where you are. Poor. Stressed. Wondering why money never works out.

The choice is yours.

This is where it starts.

PART I – Why You're Still Poor

Most people never stop to ask why they're stuck financially. They just keep moving forward, working harder, earning more, and assuming things will work out. They don't.

This section is about brutal honesty. It's about looking in the mirror and admitting the truth: you are not where you want to be with money, and there are reasons for that.

The reasons aren't hidden. They're obvious, but you've been trained to ignore them. Society pushes myths that keep you poor. The financial industry profits from your ignorance. Friends and family normalize debt and paycheck-to-paycheck living. And because everyone else is stuck too, you think it's normal.

It's not normal. It's broken.

In Part I, we're going to rip away the illusions and expose the traps that keep people poor.

- **Chapter 1: The Money Myths You Believe** breaks down the money myths you've been told: That more income is the answer, that debt is normal, that investing is gambling, that rich people are just lucky. Believing these lies is the first step to financial failure.

- **Chapter 2: Lifestyle Creep: Spending More Than You Earn** shows how lifestyle creep eats every raise and bonus until even high earners end up poor. You'll see how "I make six figures but I'm struggling" isn't a rare story, it's the standard.

- **Chapter 3: Bad Debt and Credit Addiction** pulls back the curtain on bad debt and credit addiction. You'll learn how a $5,000 balance can turn into $20,000 of pain and why the credit system is designed to keep you in held down in chains.

- **Chapter 4: No Plan, No Progress** explains why drifting without a plan guarantees zero progress. You'll meet people who made decent money for decades yet have nothing to show for it.

- **Chapter 5: The Hidden Costs of Ignorance** exposes the hidden costs of inflation, taxes, and fees. These are the forces quietly stealing from you every single day while you look the other way.

By the end of Part I, you'll understand exactly why you're not ahead financially. It will sting and it should. That pain is necessary because until you confront the problem, you'll never change it.

This isn't about guilt. This is about clarity. Once you see the problem clearly, you can fix it.

1.
The Money Myths You Believe

The lies you've been told about income, debt, luck, and investing are keeping you stuck. Expose them, reject them, and you'll see money differently forever.

Todd thought his break was coming. Every year, he went to Vegas, playing the slot machines with the same hope: "One day I'll hit it big."

He wasn't saving. He wasn't investing. He wasn't building anything. Todd wasn't chasing wealth, he was chasing luck. And luck never came. Ten years later, he was still working the same job, still struggling, and still waiting for a miracle.

Todd's story may seem extreme, but it's not. Most people aren't in Vegas every year, but they're still gambling with their financial lives. They fall for money myths that sound good, feel comfortable, or seem logical on the surface. In reality, those myths quietly drain their future.

You're not struggling because you don't work hard. You're not struggling because there isn't opportunity. You're struggling because you believe lies about money. Until you face those lies, nothing changes.

Here are the most common myths that keep people trapped.

Myth #1: More Income Will Solve It

This is the most common belief. *"If I just made more money, everything would be fine."* It feels true, because more income means more room, more choices, and more potential. But income without discipline only magnifies existing mistakes.

A 2023 LendingClub report found that **65 percent of Americans earning $100,000 or more live paycheck to paycheck.**[1] These aren't low-income households. They're six-figure earners with no cushion, no savings, and constant stress. The lifestyle looks successful on the outside, but inside the finances are fragile. Kevin is one of them. He earns $350,000 a year as a successful doctor. From the outside, he looks successful: a big house, nice cars, luxury vacations, and kids in private school. But his reality is different. His $6,000 mortgage eats one chunk. Two luxury car payments take another. Vacations go on credit cards because he "deserves them" after working so hard. Every dollar is spent before it hits his account. At tax time, he scrambles to cover his bill. At Christmas, he borrows again. He lives in the same paycheck-to-paycheck cycle as Todd, who earns $50,000 a year, only with nicer toys and higher stakes.

The truth is that income matters, but it isn't the foundation. If you can't manage $50,000 per year, you won't be able to manage $350,000 per year. In fact, the damage grows. Bigger paychecks come with bigger opportunities to overspend, to borrow, and to justify lifestyle creep. The more you earn, the easier it is to believe you can always out-earn your mistakes.

This is why you see professional athletes, celebrities, and lottery winners lose millions and end up broke. They had income beyond imagination, but no discipline, no systems, and no plan. The money amplified bad habits until the wealth disappeared.

Income is only fuel. If you have no engine, no structure, and no control, the fuel only burns faster.

Myth #2: Debt Is Normal
This belief has been sold so hard that most people no longer question it. Student loans, car loans, credit cards, and even financing furniture are treated as a standard part of life. "Everybody has debt," people say, as if it's a badge of honor.

The problem is that normal does not mean healthy. Normal is poor. Normal is stressed. Normal is handing your paycheck over to banks and lenders before you even see it.

In 2024, total U.S. household debt hit a record **$17.7 trillion**, with over **$1.1 trillion in credit card debt alone.**[2] The average household that carries a balance owes about **$6,500 at 20 percent interest.**[3] That means people are paying thousands each year just to stand still.

Remember Todd? He earns $50,000 a year and believes his problem is income, not behavior. Between his $500 car payment, $350 in student loans, and $200 in minimum credit card payments, over $1,000 of his paycheck is gone before rent, groceries, or utilities. Todd isn't unusual. He's average… Working hard, earning decently, but always running out of money before the month ends.

Debt chains you. It steals your future income before you even earn it. While some debt (like a business loan for an income-producing asset) can be strategic, most consumer debt is financial poison. If you want freedom, you have to stop normalizing debt.

Myth #3: I'll Start Saving Later
The lie of "later" ruins more futures than almost any other. People tell themselves they'll start when they get a raise, when debt is gone, or when life is less expensive. Later feels safe. Later feels rational.

Later never comes.

According to Bankrate, **22 percent of Americans have no emergency savings at all.**[4] That means nearly one in four households couldn't cover even a small setback without going into debt. For many, "later" has already run out of time.

Meanwhile, inflation quietly eats away at every dollar sitting idle. Compound interest works for those who start early, but it punishes those who delay.

Let's do the math. If you save $500 a month starting at age 25, invested at an average 7 percent per year, you will have about $1.2 million by age 65. Wait until 35, and you will have only about $580,000. Waiting ten years costs you over half a million dollars. Wait until 45, and you'll retire with barely $260,000. By then it's almost impossible to catch up without massive sacrifice.

This is why "later" is the most expensive word in personal finance. Every year you wait, the price tag goes up.

Meet Maria. In her 20s, she told herself she would save once she made more money. In her 30s, she told herself she would save once the kids were older. In her 40s, she told herself she would save once the mortgage was smaller. By 50, she had almost nothing set aside, even though she had earned millions across her career. Later stole her future.

You don't need a lot to start. You need to start with what you have right now. Even $50 a month matters because it builds the habit. Small, consistent action beats perfect timing every single time. The best time to start was yesterday. The second-best time is today.

Myth #4: Investing Is Gambling

Some people avoid investing because they think it is too risky. *"The stock market is just a casino,"* they say. Others rush in headfirst chasing crypto hype, penny stocks, or day-trading apps like they're rolling dice in Vegas. Both are wrong.

Investing is ownership. Gambling is chance.

The difference shows in the numbers. From 1928 through 2023, the S&P 500 delivered an average annual return of about **9.7 percent**, despite wars, recessions, political upheavals, inflation spikes, and market crashes.[5] That isn't luck. That's the power of compounding ownership in real companies that produce goods, employ people, and create value.

Gambling, on the other hand, is designed for you to lose. Casinos are built on negative odds. The house always wins. When you treat the stock market like a casino – jumping in and out, chasing hot tips, or betting everything on a single stock – you aren't investing. You're gambling, and the market (and your broker) becomes the house.

Crypto hype proves the point. In 2022 alone, global crypto markets lost **$2 trillion in value.**[6] Millions of people who thought they were investing discovered they were speculating. The same story repeats with meme stocks, penny stock pumps, and day-trading frenzies. A few get lucky in the short term, but most lose because they are chasing quick wins instead of building long-term ownership.

Think about it this way. When you invest $1,000 into a diversified index fund, you're buying small ownership stakes in hundreds of companies. Those companies make profits, pay dividends, and grow over time. When you throw $1,000 into a slot machine or the latest coin of the week, you own nothing. You're hoping for lightning to strike.

Investing isn't about luck or quick wins. It's about discipline, ownership, and time. The gamblers lose money. The investors build wealth.

Myth #5: Get Rich Quick

This myth sells better than any other. Social media is full of people promising shortcuts. *"Flip houses in 30 days." "Turn $100 into $10,000." "Quit your job tomorrow."* The packaging changes, but the promise is always the same: fast money with no real effort.

The results speak for themselves. Surveys show that many Americans now believe real estate flipping is a reliable way to build wealth, but the **vast majority never see real profits.**[7] Most underestimate costs, overestimate value, and lose money trying to flip what they should have held.

The same pattern repeats in crypto, multi-level marketing, penny stocks, and day-trading schemes. A few post big wins on Instagram or Reddit, but they are the exception, not the rule. The vast majority lose because they treat speculation like a shortcut instead of building a foundation.

Real wealth takes time. It takes consistent saving, disciplined investing, and smart risk-taking. It's built over years, not weeks. The shortcut mindset is dangerous because it does more than cost money. It costs time. Every year spent chasing "get rich quick" schemes is a year not spent compounding real wealth.

Meet Daniel. He works in IT and is bright and witty, but spent over a decade chasing the next hot idea – penny stocks, crypto, flipping cars, flipping houses. Every time he thought he had found the "big one," it collapsed. At 40, he realized he had wasted ten years chasing illusions while his peers who invested steadily had quietly built six-figure portfolios. His problem wasn't lack of effort. It was chasing shortcuts.

If it sounds too good to be true, it is. Shortcuts are distractions. The only proven path is time, discipline, and ownership.

Myth #6: Passive Income Fantasies
Everyone loves the phrase *"passive income."* It sounds magical. Money rolling in while you sleep. Work once, get paid forever. No boss. No schedule. Just cash flowing in while you sit on the beach.

Here's the reality. Every passive income stream requires one of three things – money, time, or risk.

- Rental properties require down payments, repairs, and tenants.
- Online businesses require marketing, content, and customer service.
- Dividend stocks require invested capital.

There's no such thing as a free stream of money.

The obsession with "passive income" has exploded in recent years, fueled by YouTube channels, Instagram reels, and TikTok influencers. Most of the people selling you on passive income are not making their money from the method they promote. They're making it from the course they sell to you. The real passive income is flowing into their pocket, not yours.

The numbers back it up. Many young adults now list "passive income" as a top financial goal, yet only a small fraction ever make any money from it. Most eventually discover that building an income stream takes far more upfront work, time, and capital than they were led to believe.

Think about Daniel. In an attempt to retire early, he spent $2,000 on an online "drop-shipping passive income" course that promised six figures in a year. Six months later, he had no sales, no profit, and a garage full of unsold gadgets he tried to resell online. Not long after, he repeated the same mistake with crypto in order to make back what he lost, chasing quick riches and losing the rest of his savings. His money never worked for him. It worked for everyone selling him the dream.

Passive income is real, but only after you put in real work or real capital. It's not a shortcut, it's a payoff.

Rental properties can generate income… but only after years of saving, buying right, and managing well.

Dividend portfolios can pay thousands a month… but only after you invest hundreds of thousands of dollars.

Online businesses can create recurring revenue… but only after years of building, testing, and scaling.

Passive income isn't magic. It's leverage. Leverage only comes after the sweat, sacrifice, and discipline most people never want to put in.

Myth #7: Rich People Are Just Lucky
This myth comforts the poor but destroys their future. *"They got lucky." "They had connections." "They were in the right place at the right time."*

Yes, luck can open doors. But wealth without discipline evaporates. A commonly cited estimate attributed to the National Endowment for Financial Education suggests that many large lottery winners **go broke within a few years.**[8] They had luck. They lacked habits.

The same is true with celebrities and athletes. Stories of people who earn tens of millions and then file for bankruptcy are everywhere. They had extraordinary income, but without systems and discipline, it all disappeared. Luck gave them a windfall, but it didn't make them wealthy.

On the other hand, most wealthy people built it deliberately. They avoided debt. They invested consistently. They tracked cash flow and lived below their means. They understood the long game. Calling it luck ignores the years of choices and discipline it took to get there.

Meet Lisa. She built a successful real estate firm over 20 years. She worked long hours, reinvested profits, and consistently saved and invested. Her neighbors said she was "lucky" to have a thriving business. But luck had nothing to do with her two decades of sacrifice, late nights, and careful money management.

Wealth is built on choices, not chance. Luck may start the story, but habits, discipline, and time finish it. If you excuse wealth as luck, you give yourself permission to stay stuck. If you accept that wealth is built, you give yourself permission to start building.

Why Myths Keep You Trapped

Every myth has a cost. Believing you just need more income makes you waste what you already have. Believing debt is normal keeps you chained to banks and lenders for life. Believing you can save later robs you of the one advantage you can't replace: **time**. Believing investing is gambling keeps you stuck on the sidelines while others compound wealth. Believing in get-rich-quick schemes wastes not only your money but also years you will never get back. Believing passive income is effortless distracts you from doing the hard work that actually produces it. Believing wealth is just luck convinces you not to try at all.

These myths feel safe because they give you excuses. They let you point the finger elsewhere: at your job, at the market, at your upbringing, at the economy… They let you say, *"It's not my fault. I'll get to it later. Someone else had an advantage I don't."* Excuses feel comfortable in the moment, but they cost you decades. While you are excusing, someone else is building.

The truth is harsh but freeing. No one is coming to save you. Not a lottery ticket, not a miracle raise, not a hot stock tip, not a secret "passive income" scheme. If you keep waiting for luck or shortcuts, you'll stay exactly where you are.

The first step to wealth is refusing to believe lies. The moment you reject myths, you gain power. You stop waiting for something magical to happen. You stop gambling on hype. You stop delaying the work. You start building systems, making disciplined choices, and putting your money to work.

That's where change begins. Not with luck. Not with fantasy. With clarity, ownership, and action.

2.
Lifestyle Creep: Spending More Than You Earn

Every raise disappears because your spending grows faster than your income. Learn why more money won't save you until you control lifestyle inflation.

Lisa used to dream about making six figures. She thought once she hit $100,000 a year, life would be different. No more stress. No more scraping by. She would finally feel secure.

When she finally reached that milestone, something strange happened. The stress didn't go away. It got worse. The new car loan. The bigger apartment. The endless meals out. Her credit card balances grew. Her savings account never grew. She had doubled her income but felt poorer than ever.

Lisa didn't fail because of income. She failed because of lifestyle creep.

What Is Lifestyle Creep?

Lifestyle creep, also called lifestyle inflation, happens when your spending rises as quickly as your income. You get a raise, a promotion, or a bonus, and instead of saving or investing the difference, you spend it.

You move into a bigger house. You buy a nicer car. You subscribe to more services. You eat out more often. You feel like you "deserve" it because you are making more. Before long, your expenses catch up to your income. You're earning more, but you're no better off.

A Forbes report explains that lifestyle inflation traps people in a cycle where every increase in earnings is matched by an increase in spending. The end result is that despite higher income, wealth never grows.[9]

This isn't just a problem for middle-income families. According to Bank of America research, about **20 percent of households earning more than $150,000 still live paycheck to paycheck.**[10] Even among top earners, mortgages, cars, insurance, and constant spending can wipe out any advantage.

Income doesn't guarantee security. If you don't control lifestyle creep, you'll always feel like you are falling behind, no matter what you earn.

Why More Income Doesn't Fix It

People assume more money will solve money problems. The truth is that without discipline, more money makes the problem bigger.

Imagine three people:

- **Person A** makes $40,000 a year. They live modestly but spend nearly everything. No savings. Always scraping by.

- **Person B** makes $100,000 a year. They upgrade their car, their housing, and their lifestyle. They also spend nearly everything. No savings. Always scraping by.

- **Person C** makes $250,000 a year. They live in a big house with a big mortgage. They drive two luxury cars. They travel. They're still living paycheck to paycheck.

The income changed. The behavior didn't. The result is the same.

A survey by PYMNTS found that even among households earning $250,000 or more, **about 40 percent were still living paycheck to paycheck**.[11] These aren't struggling families. These are high earners who allowed lifestyle creep to consume every dollar.

If you don't control your money now, more income will only speed up the damage.

How Lifestyle Creep Works

Lifestyle creep doesn't happen all at once. *It sneaks up on you.*

You get a small raise and upgrade your phone.

Another raise, and you upgrade your car.

Another bonus, and you move into a bigger apartment or house.

You start adding subscriptions. Streaming services. Gym memberships. Meal kits.

Each choice feels small. None of them seem like a big deal. But together, they add up to hundreds or even thousands of dollars a month. Before long, every dollar is spoken for.

The scariest part is that lifestyle creep feels normal. Society tells you that spending more is a sign of success. Ads tell you that you deserve better. Friends and family reinforce it. You believe you're moving up in the world, when in reality, you're standing still.

The Psychology of Lifestyle Creep
Lifestyle creep isn't just math. *It's mindset.*

Humans adapt quickly. What once felt like a luxury becomes an expectation. The first time you buy a new car, it feels exciting. Two years later, you're itching for another upgrade. The apartment that once felt huge starts feeling small. The vacation that felt incredible now feels standard.

Psychologists call this the **hedonic treadmill**. You work harder, earn more, and spend more, but your satisfaction never increases. You're running faster but not getting anywhere.

The problem isn't that you want nice things. The problem is that you convince yourself you can't live without them.

Real Numbers: $40K vs $100K vs $250K
Let's break this down with numbers.

- **At $40,000 a year** (~$3,333 a month take-home), you rent a modest apartment, drive a used car, and eat out occasionally. You spend nearly everything. Savings: $0.

- **At $100,000 a year** (~$6,667 a month take-home), you move into a $2,500-a-month apartment, buy a $600 car, add streaming services, eat out 3-4 nights a week, and take nicer vacations. You spend nearly everything. Savings: $0.

- **At $250,000 a year** (~$14,000 a month take-home), you buy a $1 million house with a $6,000 mortgage, drive two luxury cars, spend $2,000 on travel, $1,500 on dining, and hundreds more on subscriptions and shopping. You spend nearly everything. Savings: $0.

The income doubled, then doubled again. The result stayed the same. No cushion. No freedom. No wealth.

How to Spot Lifestyle Creep
You may already be in it without realizing it. Here are the signs:

- You make more money than ever but still feel financially stressed.
- Your savings account never grows.
- You justify every upgrade as something you "deserve."
- Your monthly payments rise every year.
- You would be in trouble if your paycheck stopped for even one month.

If that describes you, you're not alone. Millions are in the same trap. But you don't have to stay there.

How to Reverse Lifestyle Creep
Reversing lifestyle creep is not about depriving yourself. It's about reclaiming control.

1. **Track your spending.** You can't change what you don't measure. Write down every subscription, payment, and expense. The truth will shock you.

2. **Set a savings rate.** Decide on a percentage of your income that will always go to savings or investments first. Ten percent, fifteen percent, twenty percent. Automate it.

3. **Delay upgrades.** When you get a raise, keep your lifestyle the same for at least six months. Bank the difference.

4. **Kill subscriptions.** Cancel what you don't use. Bundle where possible. Stop paying for things that don't matter.

5. **Redefine success.** Stop equating luxury with wealth. Real wealth is freedom, not payments.

Break the Cycle

Lifestyle creep is a silent thief. It disguises itself as progress, but it keeps you stuck. More money doesn't equal more wealth. Without discipline, more money only creates more stress.

If you want to be wealthy, you need to live below your means. Not forever, but long enough to create a cushion. Cushion creates savings. Savings create investments. Investments create freedom.

The people who build wealth aren't always the ones who earn the most. They're the ones who resist the pull of lifestyle creep. They use raises to buy freedom, not payments. They choose cushion over image.

Will your next raise make you richer, or just busier paying bills? The choice is yours.

3.
Bad Debt and Credit Addiction

Credit feels like freedom, but it's the fastest path to chains. Understand how debt steals your future and how to finally break out.

Meet Maya. She was drowning in credit card bills. It started with a $2,000 balance she thought she would "pay off next month." That was three years ago. Now her balance is $8,000. She makes minimum payments, but the balance never seems to go down. In fact, it keeps going up.

Her story isn't unusual. Credit card companies know how to trap people. They offer easy credit, low introductory rates, and small minimum payments. They don't need you to pay off your balance. In fact, they make billions when you don't.

Debt isn't just a financial burden. It's a system designed to keep you stuck.

The Real Cost of Credit Card Debt

Most credit cards carry interest rates around 20 percent. According to the Federal Reserve, the average APR on interest-accruing credit cards hit **20.6 percent in 2023**, the highest on record.[13]

What does that mean for you? If you carry a $5,000 balance and only make minimum payments, you could pay back $15,000 or more over time. In some cases, it can take 20 years to pay off a single balance. That's money you'll never get back, money that could have been invested, saved, or used to build something real.

The trap is in the minimum payment. Credit card statements often show a "minimum due" of $100 or $150. Paying that amount feels manageable. What you don't see is that most of that payment goes to interest, not principal. The balance barely moves, and you stay trapped.

How Debt Spirals Form

Debt rarely starts with one big mistake. It builds slowly, then snowballs. Here are some of the most common traps:

Balance Transfers

A balance transfer looks like relief. A zero percent introductory rate sounds like freedom. Credit card companies know exactly how tempting this feels when you are drowning in debt. They make it sound like a reset button. Move your balance here, pay no interest, and you'll finally get ahead.

But here's the trap: the promotional period is short, often 12 to 18 months. If you haven't paid the balance down before it ends, the interest rate doesn't just return to normal. It skyrockets. In many cases, it jumps even higher than the card you left. Some cards even apply the new rate to the entire transferred balance, not just what remains. Suddenly, what felt like relief becomes a deeper hole.

It gets worse. Every balance transfer usually comes with a transfer fee, often 3 to 5 percent of the amount moved. That means if you transfer $10,000, you could pay $300 to $500 just for the privilege of shifting debt around. You haven't solved the problem. You've paid for the illusion of solving it.

Because the new card feels like a fresh start, many people make the classic mistake of using the old card again. Now instead of one balance, they have two. Instead of progress, they have doubled the problem.

A balance transfer without a strict payoff plan isn't a solution. It's procrastination with fees attached. If you don't change the habits that created the debt, the transfer only delays the pain and makes the final bill worse.

Payday Loans

Payday lenders target people in financial stress. They promise quick relief. Cash today, no questions asked. To someone desperate to cover rent or a car payment, it feels like a lifeline. In reality, it's a trap.

According to the Consumer Financial Protection Bureau, the average annual percentage rate on payday loans is about **400 percent.**[14] That means borrowing $500 isn't a favor. It's a financial time bomb. Within weeks, that $500 can balloon into $750, $1,000, or more after fees and rollovers pile up.

Here's how it works: most payday loans are due in two weeks. But when the deadline arrives, the borrower often can't pay the full balance, so they "roll over" the loan into a new one. Each rollover adds another round of fees. The debt multiplies. What began as $500 can snowball into thousands.

The lenders know it. Their business model depends on repeat borrowers. They don't make money when you pay the loan off quickly. They make money when you can't. That's why payday lenders cluster in low-income neighborhoods and advertise heavily to people who are already struggling.

Payday loans aren't a bridge. They're a sinkhole. Once you step in, you sink deeper each time you roll it over. If you're ever tempted by one, stop and ask yourself: will this solve the problem, or will it just add another? The answer is almost always the latter.

Buy Now, Pay Later (BNPL)
"Buy now, pay later" is the new credit card. Companies like Klarna, Afterpay, and Affirm make it simple to split a purchase into installments. To the consumer, it feels painless. The $200 pair of shoes suddenly looks like four easy payments of $50. The $1,200 laptop feels more affordable when broken into $100 chunks. It tricks your brain into thinking you're spending less, when in reality you're spending the same amount, only with added risk.

The danger is that BNPL encourages overspending. When you can chop every purchase into smaller pieces, you stop feeling the weight of the total. You tell yourself, "It's only $40 this month," but forget that you signed up for five other "only $40" payments last week. Those little installments stack up until you are juggling dozens of obligations at once.

This is how it spirals. You finance clothes on one app, electronics on another, and household items on a third. Each purchase feels small, but together they add up to hundreds of dollars in automatic withdrawals hitting your account at different times of the month. You lose track of which payment is due where. Miss one, and you're hit with late fees. Miss more, and interest charges pile on. What began as "easy" turns into a web of small debts that are harder to escape than a single large bill.

BNPL isn't harmless. It's debt disguised as convenience. These companies know most people won't track every micro-payment, and they count on it. They profit when consumers overextend themselves and slip into the cycle of fees. If you can't afford to pay for something today, stretching it into tomorrow does not make it affordable. It just makes it debt.

The Cycle

It rarely starts as a disaster. It begins with one credit card. A small balance at first. Then another card, because the first one is maxed out. Then a payday loan to cover a bill that couldn't wait. Then a balance transfer that feels like relief but only delays the pain. Then a buy now, pay later plan for something you convinced yourself you needed.

Before long, you aren't managing money anymore. You're managing debt. One payment comes due, and the only way to make it is to borrow from somewhere else. You take a cash advance on one card to cover the minimum on another. You use a balance transfer to buy time but never reduce the balance. You roll over a payday loan because you can't cover it in two weeks. You keep stacking BNPL purchases until you lose track of how many small payments are coming out of your account each month.

This is the cycle. You aren't building wealth. You're shuffling debt. You're not moving forward. You're running in place while the ground beneath you gets softer. The more you try to juggle, the heavier it becomes, and eventually you drop everything at once.

The cycle thrives on two things, avoidance and hope. Avoidance makes you push off the pain by moving balances around instead of paying them down. Hope convinces you that the next paycheck, the next promotion, or the next tax refund will solve it. But the math doesn't care about hope. The interest keeps growing. The payments keep multiplying.

Once you're in the cycle, there's no coasting. You're either climbing out with discipline and sacrifice, or you're sinking deeper. There is no middle ground.

Case Study: $5,000 Becomes $20,000
Let's do the math.

If you carry a $5,000 credit card balance at 20 percent interest and only make minimum payments (let's say 2 percent of the balance), it could take more than 20 years to pay it off. Over that time, you would pay about $20,000 total.

Think about that. A $5,000 purchase becomes a $20,000 mistake. And the bank profits every step of the way.

Now imagine carrying not just one balance, but three or four cards. That is how people end up buried in $20,000, $40,000, even $100,000 of unsecured debt.

Why Debt Feels Addictive
Debt isn't just numbers. It feels addictive because it plays on psychology.

- **Easy access.** Credit cards are mailed to you. Payday lenders are on every corner. BNPL is built into online checkout. It takes seconds to borrow.

- **Small payments.** Minimums make you feel like you are managing. A $50 payment doesn't hurt, so you don't feel urgency to pay it off.

- **Illusion of control.** You convince yourself you are "handling it" because payments are being made. In reality, the balance is barely moving.

- **Temporary relief.** Debt feels like a solution in the moment. It covers bills, emergencies, or wants. But the relief is temporary, and the pain is long-term.

Credit addiction isn't about liking debt. It's about using it as a crutch to cover short-term needs without facing long-term consequences.

The Hidden Cost of Debt
Debt doesn't just cost you money. It costs you freedom.

- **Lost opportunity.** Every dollar in interest is a dollar you could have invested.

- **Stress.** Studies show that debt is one of the top causes of anxiety and relationship conflicts.

- **Reduced options.** Debt limits your ability to take risks, invest in opportunities, or even switch jobs.

- **Future wealth destroyed.** Carrying balances into your 30s, 40s, or 50s means decades of compounding are lost.

The average American household with credit card debt pays over **$1,380 a year in interest alone**.[15] That's a mortgage payment, a quick vacation, or a start to an investment account. Instead, it goes to the bank.

Using Credit as a Tool, Not a Lifeline
Credit itself isn't evil. Used wisely, it's a valuable tool. It can help you build a credit score, qualify for a mortgage, or leverage rewards. The problem is when credit becomes a lifeline.

- **Tool:** You use credit to earn points, then pay it off in full each month.

- **Lifeline:** You swipe to cover bills, then carry the balance for years.

- **Tool:** You finance a mortgage to buy a home that builds equity.
- **Lifeline:** You finance vacations, gadgets, or luxuries that lose value.

The difference is discipline. A tool builds your future. A lifeline drains it.

How to Break Free

Escaping bad debt requires action, not hope. There's no shortcut. You can't wish it away, refinance it into oblivion, or wait for a miracle raise. The only way out is to face it head-on and attack it with discipline. Here's how:

1. Face the numbers.

Denial keeps you stuck. Until you see the full picture, you can't fix it. Write down every single balance, every interest rate, and every minimum payment. Do not round down. Do not guess. Put the real numbers in front of you, even if it feels painful. Clarity hurts in the moment, but it gives you power. You can't defeat what you refuse to measure.

2. Choose a method.

Once you know the numbers, you need a plan. There are two proven methods:

- **Debt snowball:** Pay off the smallest balance first, then roll that payment into the next one. This gives quick wins and builds momentum.

- **Debt avalanche:** Pay off the highest interest rate first, then move down. This saves the most money long-term.

Both methods work fine. The "best" one is the one you'll actually follow. Pick one and commit. The danger is switching back and forth or trying to reinvent the wheel. Consistency beats cleverness.

3. Cut the cards.

Stop the bleeding. If you keep borrowing, you'll never escape. Put the credit cards away. Cancel buy now, pay later plans. Stop payday loan rollovers. Close the traps one by one. Debt is like a fire. You can't put it out while you keep pouring gasoline on it. Cutting off the inflow is non-negotiable.

4. Build an emergency fund.

Debt keeps coming back because life keeps happening. A car repair, a medical bill, or a broken appliance sends people right back to the card. The only way to break the cycle is to have cash ready.

Even $500 set aside is enough to stop one crisis from putting you back in the hole. As you pay down debt, grow this fund to one month, then three months of expenses. This isn't optional. This is your shield.

5. Automate payments.

Willpower fails. Systems win. Automate your payments so they happen whether you think about them or not. Always pay more than the minimum, even if it's only $25 more. Every extra dollar cuts down interest and shortens the timeline. Automation keeps you from backsliding, missing due dates, or convincing yourself to "skip this month."

Breaking free won't happen overnight. You didn't get into debt overnight, and you won't get out of it in a weekend. But every dollar you pay off is a dollar you reclaim for your future. Every card you close is a chain broken. The process may take months or years, but once you are free, you stay free – and the money that was once going to banks now stays with you.

Debt Is Not Wealth

Bad debt is the opposite of wealth. It steals your future, traps your income, and transfers your money to lenders.

Credit can be a powerful tool when used wisely, but it's never a lifeline. If you rely on credit to survive, you're sinking, not swimming.

The good news is you can break free. You can pay it off. You can live without it. And when you do, the stress lifts, the cushion grows, and real wealth begins.

4.
No Plan, No Progress

Wandering without a budget or goals guarantees the same results: nothing. Wealth starts with a plan, not a paycheck.

Daniel was doing well. He earned $80,000 a year, had steady raises, and lived in a nice apartment. He never felt rich, but he never felt poor either. He assumed that as long as he kept working hard, everything else would fall into place. Ten years later, he looked at his finances and was shocked. His net worth was zero. A decade of income had come and gone, and he had nothing to show for it.

Daniel's mistake was not laziness. He worked hard, paid his bills, and kept moving forward. His mistake was drifting. He never had a plan. He never set goals, tracked spending, or built a system. He thought making decent money was enough. It wasn't.

This is the cost of living without a financial plan.

Why No Plan Means No Progress

Money doesn't grow by accident. Without a plan, it slips through your hands. Bills, lifestyle creep, and unexpected expenses consume everything you earn. A raise disappears as quickly as it arrives. A bonus is spent before it even clears the bank. What feels like progress turns into another cycle of paycheck-to-paycheck stress.

A 2023 Gallup poll found that only **32 percent of Americans keep a household budget.**[16] That means two-thirds of households are flying blind. They have no idea where their money is going. They work hard, they earn income, but they never see the results because they never tell their money where to go.

This is why so many people say, "I make good money, but I have nothing to show for it." Without a plan, more income doesn't fix the problem. It just creates more ways to spend.

Think about it. You plan vacations. You plan meals. You plan weddings, workouts, and weekends. Yet most people refuse to plan the very thing that determines whether they can ever retire, buy a home, or stop living under constant stress. That's why they stay stuck.

Without a plan, progress is impossible. You may feel busy. You may feel productive. You may even feel like you're "working on it." But without a budget, without a target, you're running in place. Activity without direction is wasted effort.

If you want progress, you need a plan. Even a simple one. A plan gives your money purpose. It tells your dollars where to go instead of wondering where they went.

The Cost of Drifting: Stories That Prove the Point
Daniel at $80K. A decade of earning with no plan left him with nothing.

Maya at $50K. She lived modestly, paid her rent, and managed her bills. But she never tracked her spending. She told herself she would start saving "next year." Fifteen years later, she had no retirement account, $12,000 in credit card debt, and constant stress about money.

Kevin at $350K. A successful professional, Kevin assumed his high income meant he was secure. He never tracked net worth or set goals. He had a $6,000 mortgage payment, two leased cars, and no investments outside his 401(k). At age 45, he realized he had been working for 20 years and had less than $50,000 in liquid savings.

Different incomes. Same problem. No plan.

The Illusion of "Doing Okay"
The danger of drifting is that it feels safe. You pay your bills. You make your minimum payments. You keep the lights on and the car running. You convince yourself you're "doing okay." You tell yourself that as long as you're not behind, everything is fine.

But "okay" is an illusion. "Okay" means fragile. "Okay" means you're one job loss, one medical bill, or one recession away from a full-blown crisis.

A 2023 Federal Reserve report found that nearly **40 percent of adults could not cover a $400 emergency expense without borrowing or selling something.**[17] That includes millions of people with good jobs, steady paychecks, and even nice houses or cars. They're not fine. They're fragile. Their "okay" can collapse at any moment with one surprise expense.

Think about what "okay" looks like in practice. You earn $70,000. You have a car payment, rent or a mortgage, subscriptions, eating out, a vacation or two. You aren't drowning, but you're not saving either. Then the transmission fails. Or your child needs medical care. Or your company announces layoffs. Suddenly your entire sense of stability shatters because there was no cushion.

This is why drifting is dangerous. It doesn't feel like failure, so you don't change. You keep telling yourself you're fine until the storm comes. When it does, you find out you weren't fine at all.

Daniel thought he was fine. He made his payments, but one medical bill buried him in credit card debt. Kevin thought he was fine. When his hours were cut, he couldn't keep up and lost his car. Maya thought she was fine. When her landlord raised the rent, she had no savings to cover the move. None of them were fine. They were fragile, and fragile always breaks under pressure.

If your financial life can collapse from one unexpected event, you're not "okay." You're at risk. Real security does not come from paying the bills on time. It comes from a cushion, savings, and systems that keep you steady no matter what life throws your way.

Why Planning Matters More Than Income
Income matters, but planning matters more.

- Someone earning $60,000 who saves 20 percent will build wealth faster than someone earning $150,000 who saves only 5 percent.

- Someone tracking net worth will see progress and adjust course. Someone drifting will wake up 10 years later with nothing.

- Planning multiplies the effect of income. Drifting erases it.

A Charles Schwab survey found that **those with a written financial plan are more likely to save regularly, pay bills on time, and feel confident about reaching their goals.**[18] Planning changes behavior. Behavior changes results.

The Building Blocks of a Plan
A financial plan doesn't need to be complicated. At its core, it's supported by three building blocks:

1. Cash Flow
Money in, money out. Do you know how much you spend each month? Most people don't. Tracking cash flow exposes leaks. It shows you where your dollars are going and whether your lifestyle is sustainable.

Tools:
- Old school: pen and paper.
- Spreadsheets: simple Excel or Google Sheets.
- Apps: YNAB (You Need a Budget), EveryDollar, Tiller.

The method matters less than the awareness.

2. Savings Rate
What percentage of your income do you save or invest? Ten percent is a start. Fifteen percent is better. Twenty percent or more builds wealth faster.

Savings rate matters more than income. Someone who saves 20 percent of $60,000 ($12,000/year) will surpass someone who saves 5 percent of $150,000 ($7,500/year).

3. Net Worth
Assets minus liabilities. What you own minus what you owe. Net worth is the scoreboard of financial progress. It doesn't lie.

Tracking net worth quarterly forces you to face the truth. You may have high income but negative net worth if you have more debt than assets. The goal is to see the number grow steadily over time.

The Hidden Costs of Not Planning
The cost of drifting isn't just zero progress. It's negative progress. When you fail to plan, money doesn't stay neutral. It leaks, it shrinks, and it disappears. Here's what happens:

- **Missed Compounding.** Every year you wait to invest costs you tens or even hundreds of thousands of dollars. Compounding is a clock that never stops ticking. Start at 25 and you could retire a multi-millionaire. Wait until 35 and you may end up with less than half a million, even if you contribute the same amount. Delay has a price, and it's expensive.

- **Permanent Debt.** Without a plan, debt lingers for decades. You make minimum payments, shift balances around, and convince yourself you are "managing it." But without a plan to pay it off, you're trapped. What began as a $5,000 balance can end up costing $20,000 or more in interest over time. Debt without a plan isn't temporary. It's permanent.

- **Retirement Shortfalls.** Fidelity estimates the average 65-year-old today needs **$1.7 million** to retire comfortably.[19] Most households are nowhere close. They arrive at 60 and realize they never saved enough because they never had a plan. At that point, catching up is almost impossible. The years they wasted can't be replaced.

- **Stress and Regret.** Financial stress is one of the top causes of divorce and anxiety.[20] It eats away at marriages, ruins health, and keeps people awake at night. People who drift often don't connect their stress to their lack of planning. They think it is just "life being hard," when in reality it's the weight of years of financial neglect weighing down on them.

Drifting isn't safe. It's not neutral. It's expensive. A plan isn't optional if you want freedom. Without one, you're quietly digging a hole you may never climb out of.

How to Start Planning

1. **Face Reality.** Write down your income, expenses, debts, and assets. See the whole picture. Be honest.

2. **Pick One Goal.** Pay off a card. Save $1,000. Build momentum.

3. **Decide a Savings Rate.** Choose a percentage you can commit to. Automate it.

4. **Track Net Worth.** Update every three months. Watch the line move upward.

5. **Adjust Annually.** Review your plan once a year and make changes.

Planning Methods That Work

- **The Half Rule.** Save at least half of what you make. Use the remaining half for everything else. This guarantees financial stability no matter your situation because you're always living below your means (more on this in Chapter 7.)

- **Zero-Based Budget.** Every dollar gets a job. Nothing left unassigned. This forces you to make intentional decisions instead of letting money slip away.

- **Pay Yourself First.** Automate savings before spending anything else. When savings is treated as the first bill, you build wealth consistently instead of hoping there is something left over.

Different systems work for different people. What matters is using a system instead of drifting.

Why Planning Beats Luck

Some people drift because they believe something will bail them out. An inheritance. A lottery win. A promotion. A windfall. They convince themselves that one big event will solve everything.

But luck isn't a strategy. Inheritances can disappear in months without a plan. Lottery winners go broke because they never learned how to manage money. Promotions add income but also tempt bigger spending. A windfall without structure evaporates.

Planning beats luck every single time. A person who saves and invests $200 a month with discipline will outpace the person who waits for a miracle that never comes. Luck may show up, but it's unreliable. A plan, followed over years, works every time.

The Cost of Waiting

Every year you wait to plan, the cost grows. Compounding is unforgiving.

If you save $500 a month starting at 25, invested at 7 percent, you will have about $1.2 million by 65. Start at 35, and you will have only $567,000. Start at 45, and you will retire with just $258,000. Waiting a decade to save just cost you more than half a million dollars. Waiting two decades cost you nearly a million.

This is why time is the most valuable financial resource you have. You can earn more money, but you can't earn more years. Delay is expensive, and most people gravely underestimate just how expensive it is. The sooner you plan, the easier it gets. The later you start, the more extreme the sacrifices need to become.

Drift or Drive

Without a plan, you drift. You work hard for decades but look back at 50 or 60 and wonder where it all went. The money passed through your hands. The years passed too. Drifting is activity without direction. It feels busy, but it produces nothing lasting.

With a plan, you drive. You set goals, track progress, and adjust course along the way. You know where you're going, and you measure each step. You still face challenges, but you face them with clarity and control.

Drift for another decade and stay in the same place, or take the wheel now and build a future worth having. One path ends in regret. The other ends in freedom.

5.
The Hidden Costs of Ignorance

Inflation, taxes, and fees are silent killers of wealth. What you don't know about money is costing you every day.

Meet Maria. She thought she was being smart. She saved $10,000 in the bank and left it there. She called it her "nest egg" and felt proud that she never touched it. For years she believed that money was safe.

But ten years later, she was shocked. Prices had gone up, but her savings had not. What used to buy $10,000 worth of goods could now only buy about $7,500. Her money didn't grow. It lost value while it sat still.

What happened? Inflation, taxes, and hidden fees.

Ignorance is expensive. What you don't know about money quietly eats away at your wealth every single day. You don't see it. You don't feel it immediately. But over time, it robs you of freedom.

This chapter exposes the three silent killers of wealth: inflation, taxes, and fees. Once you understand them, you can defend yourself. Until then, they will quietly drain you.

1. Inflation: The Silent Thief

Most people think of inflation as just "prices going up." Gas costs more. Groceries cost more. Rent goes up. But the deeper reality is this: every year, your money buys less. Inflation quietly erodes your wealth without you ever spending a dime. You may feel like you're standing still, but you're actually sliding backward.

Why Inflation Happens

Inflation happens when the supply of money grows faster than the supply of goods and services. When more dollars are chasing the same amount of goods, prices rise. Central banks like the Federal Reserve try to control inflation by adjusting interest rates. Raise rates, and borrowing slows down because loans become more expensive. Cut rates, and money flows more easily into the economy.

But no matter how it's managed, some level of inflation always exists. It's built into the system. That's why a burger that cost $0.15 in the 1950s now costs $8 or more today. The dollar has less purchasing power with each passing year.

The Numbers

Inflation may sound small when quoted as a percentage, but the math is brutal.

- At **3 percent inflation**, $100 loses nearly half its value in 25 years.
- At **5 percent inflation**, $100 shrinks to just $38 in 25 years.
- At **9 percent inflation** (like in 2022), money lost value so fast it was almost visible month to month.

The Bureau of Labor Statistics reported that prices in the U.S. increased more in 2022 than in any year since 1981.[22] Anyone sitting on large amounts of cash that year watched their "safe" money get destroyed in real time.

Why It Matters

This is why sitting on cash isn't safety. It's risk. Inflation guarantees that money kept idle will lose power. A $50,000 savings account that looks solid today may only buy $30,000 worth of goods twenty years from now.

People think savings accounts are "safe." Safe from market crashes, yes. But not safe from inflation. If your bank account pays 0.5 percent interest while inflation runs at 3 percent, your money is shrinking by 2.5 percent every year. That's like a slow leak in your financial tire.

Without growth, your future is quietly being eaten away in the background.

Investing isn't optional in an inflationary world. You don't have to gamble, but you do have to grow. If your money isn't earning more than inflation, you're moving backward whether you like it or not.

Beating Inflation

You don't fight inflation by wishing it away. You fight it by owning assets that grow faster than inflation:

- **Stocks.** Over the long term, stocks have returned around 9–10 percent annually.
- **Real Estate.** Property values and rents rise along with inflation, making real estate a natural hedge.
- **Businesses.** Ownership in productive companies creates wealth that outpaces rising costs.

Cash is for emergencies. Investments are for growth. If you want to build wealth, you can't afford to let inflation eat your future while your money sits idle.

2. Taxes: The Cost You Can't Ignore

Taxes are another silent wealth killer. You see them on your paycheck, but you may not see how much they cost you over a lifetime.

How Taxes Work

Every dollar you earn is taxed. Income tax, payroll tax, sales tax, property tax... Even when you invest, gains are taxed. Without planning, taxes take far more than they need to.

- **Federal Income Tax:** Based on your income bracket.
- **Payroll Tax:** Funds Social Security and Medicare.
- **State and Local Taxes:** Depends where you live.
- **Capital Gains Tax:** Paid when you sell investments for a profit.
- **Dividend and Interest Taxes:** Paid on investment income.

The Numbers

The Tax Policy Center reports that the average American household paid about **13.6 percent of its income in federal taxes in 2021.**[23] That doesn't include payroll, state, or sales taxes. Add everything up, and the real tax burden is much higher.

For high earners, ignorance costs even more. Without tax planning, a $200,000 earner can lose 35–40 percent of their income to taxes. Over a 40-year career, that's millions gone.

The Retirement Tax Trap

Many people save diligently in 401(k)s or IRAs without ever realizing how taxes will hit them later. They look at their statement and think, *"I have a million dollars saved."* But that number isn't quite real.

Every dollar in a traditional 401(k) or IRA is taxable when you take it out. Depending on your tax bracket in retirement, that "million" might only be worth $700,000 or less. For some, it could be closer to $600,000. Ignorance of tax implications creates a false sense of security.

This is why so many retirees feel blindsided. They thought they were prepared, only to find out that Uncle Sam (the IRS) had been a silent partner in their retirement account all along.

The Ignorance Penalty

The wealthy avoid overpaying taxes not because they cheat, but because they plan. They use the rules to their advantage. Retirement accounts, health savings accounts (HSAs), Roth conversions, trusts, and business structures are tools available to anyone. The difference is that wealthy people use them while the average person ignores them.

Most people simply let taxes happen. They earn, they pay, they invest blindly, and they repeat. Year after year, they hand over money they could have kept. Not because they had to, but because they did not know any better. That's the ignorance penalty: paying more than you should simply because you didn't plan.

Example: Taxable vs. Tax-Free Growth
- Maria decided to invest her $10,000 in a taxable brokerage account. Over time, it doubles to $20,000. When she sells, she owes 15 percent capital gains tax, which is $1,500. Her real profit is $8,500.

- What if she invested $10,000 in a Roth IRA instead? Invested exactly the same as the taxable account, it also doubles to $20,000. When she sells in retirement, she owes $0 in taxes. Her real profit is $10,000.

Same growth. Same investment. But in a Roth IRA, she keeps more because she used the right account. Maria paid $1,500 to the IRS in her taxable account for no reason other than lack of planning.

Why This Matters

Over a single investment, $1,500 may not sound life-changing. But multiply that across decades of contributions, market growth, and withdrawals, and the difference can be hundreds of thousands of dollars. Taxes compound just like investments do. Without a strategy, you compound losses instead of gains.

Retirement security isn't just about saving. It's about knowing how much of that savings you actually get to keep. If you don't understand the tax rules, you'll spend your golden years giving away money you could have protected.

3. Fees: The Hidden Drain

The third silent killer is fees. Unlike taxes and inflation, some fees are avoidable. Others are worth every penny if they actually add value. The problem is that most people never stop to measure what they are paying or what they are getting in return.

Banking Fees

Banks make billions off their customers from avoidable charges. Overdrafts, ATM fees, account maintenance – it adds up. In 2022, Americans paid more than $8 billion in overdraft fees.[24] That's money lost not because of bad luck, but because people weren't paying attention. A simple shift to the right account or keeping a small cushion of cash can eliminate most of these costs.

Investment Fees

Over time, fees can quietly destroy wealth. A 1 percent annual fee may not sound like much, but over 30 years it can consume more than 25 percent of your total returns. Add in layered fund costs or hidden commissions, and decades of compounding get siphoned away before you even see the results.

Let's make one thing clear, not all fees are bad. A strong investment advisor who builds a plan that consistently outperforms the market net of fees, or who helps you avoid costly mistakes, is worth the price. Good advice can more than pay for itself in higher returns, smarter tax planning, and better risk management.

Consider this example. An advisor charges 1.5 percent in fees but helps you earn 10 percent when the general market is only returning 7 percent. Even after paying the fee, your net return is 8.5 percent – far stronger than the market average. The value added by good advice is what matters, not the headline fee alone.

The real danger is paying high fees for products that underperform and add no real value. Many investors are steered into **predatory annuities and insurance-based products** that promise safety and growth but bury layers of costs inside the fine print. Commissions, surrender charges, and hidden expenses quietly eat away returns year after year. These products are sold aggressively because they are profitable for the salesperson, not because they are good for the investor.[25]

For example, take $500,000 invested for 30 years:

- **1% Fee with Market 7% Returns**: Portfolio grows to about **$2.87 million**. The steady growth is strong, but fees still take a slice over time.

- **3% Annuity Fee with Market 7% Returns**: Portfolio ends with only **$1.62 million**. The extra drag cuts your wealth almost in half.

- **1.5% Advisor Fee with 10% Returns**: Portfolio grows to about **$5.78 million**. Even with higher fees, stronger performance and smart planning create far more wealth.

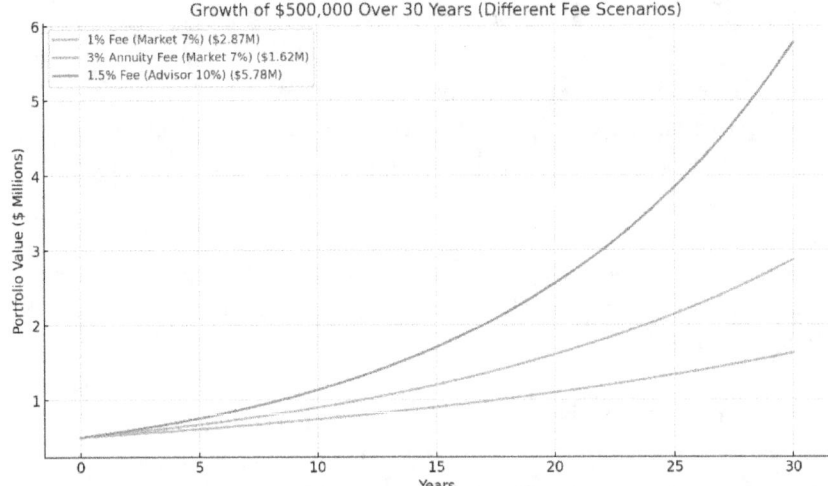

Figure: The Real Cost of Fees Over 30 Years
Starting with $500,000, a 1% market fee grows to $2.87M, a 3% annuity fee drags you down to $1.62M, while a 1.5% advisor fee with higher returns builds $5.78M.

Fees are not the enemy. Useless fees are. The smart move is to cut products and costs that destroy wealth while being willing to pay for guidance and strategy that grow it.

The Hidden Costs Compound
Inflation, taxes, and fees are bad enough individually. Together, they are devastating.

- Inflation silently eats your purchasing power.
- Taxes silently reduce your earnings and investment growth.
- Fees silently drain your returns.

Each year may not seem like much. But compounded over decades, ignorance costs millions.

Case Study:
- **Investor A** saves $5,000 a year for 30 years in a taxable annuity charging 3 percent in annual fees. After inflation,

taxes, and ongoing costs, the account ends with roughly $250,000 in real purchasing power.

- **Investor B** saves the same $5,000 a year for 30 years in a Roth IRA invested in a low-cost index fund. After inflation, the balance grows to about $400,000 in real purchasing power.

Same income. Same savings. Different strategy. **Investor B** keeps about **$150,000 more** simply by avoiding high fees and using a tax-efficient account.

Why Ignorance Persists

Why do people ignore inflation, taxes, and fees?

- **They are invisible.** Inflation doesn't send a bill. Fees hide in fine print. Taxes are withheld automatically.

- **They feel small.** A 1 percent fee seems harmless. A $3 ATM fee feels trivial. But over time, they add up.

- **They seem complicated.** Many believe only experts can understand these concepts.

These forces are simple once explained. And the cost of not learning them is enormous.

Financial Literacy Pays

The opposite of ignorance is literacy. Financial literacy turns invisible costs into manageable numbers.

- Understanding inflation motivates you to invest.
- Understanding taxes motivates you to plan and use the right accounts.
- Understanding fees motivates you to demand value.

A FINRA study found that **financially literate people are more likely to plan for retirement, have emergency savings, and avoid high-cost debt**.[26] Literacy translates into wealth.

Ignorance Is Expensive

Maria thought her savings were safe. They weren't. Millions think inflation, taxes, and fees don't matter. They do.

Ignorance is expensive. It quietly drains you every year. But financial literacy pays. Every time you learn, plan, and act, you keep more of your money.

Stay ignorant and keep losing, or get informed and start winning.

PART II –
What To Do
About It

Now you know why you're stuck. You've learned the myths, the debt traps, the lack of planning, and the hidden costs that eat away at your future.

Awareness is only the first step. If you stop here, you stay stuck. Part II shows you how to move forward.

This section is about building. It's about taking control and creating the habits, systems, and strategies that actually work in the real world.

Forget the noise you've heard before. Forget the one-size-fits-all advice that hasn't worked for you. What you're about to read isn't theory. It's not about "maybe someday." It's about what you can do right now.

In Part II you will learn:

- **Chapter 6: The Wealth Mindset Shift** shows how to shift your mindset. Wealth starts in your head before it shows up in your bank account. If you think like everyone else, you'll stay stuck like everyone else.

- **Chapter 7: Cash Flow is King** shows how to master cash flow. This isn't about restriction. It's about freedom. When you control your money, you control your life.

- **Chapter 8: Kill the Bad Debt, Build Good Credit** shows how to destroy bad debt while building good credit. Credit is a tool, but only if you use it strategically.

- **Chapter 9: Investing That Actually Works** shows how to invest in ways that actually work. You'll learn why real investing isn't gambling and how compounding can build lasting wealth.

- **Chapter 10: Build Multiple Streams of Income** shows how to build multiple streams of income. Relying on one paycheck is dangerous. Wealthy people diversify income, and you will too.

- **Chapter 11: Taxes, Protection, and Smart Structures** shows how to protect what you build. Taxes, insurance, and legal structures might not sound exciting, but they're the armor that protects your wealth from being wiped out.

By the end of Part II, you won't just know what to do – you'll have a plan you can put into action.

This is where drifting ends. This is where excuses die. This is where you stop being controlled by money and start controlling it.

6.
The Wealth Mindset Shift

Wealth is built in your head before it shows up in your bank account. Shift from scarcity to abundance and see money as a tool, not a trap.

Wealth is built in your head before it ever shows up in your bank account. If you think poor, you stay poor. If you think wealthy, you build wealth.

Money isn't just numbers on a spreadsheet. It's a mindset. The way you think about money determines the way you use it. The way you use it determines whether you end up poor or financially free.

You can't build wealth with the same mindset that kept you stuck. You need to shift how you see money, how you react to it, and how you decide with it. Wealth begins as a thought, then becomes a habit, then becomes a reality.

Most people never make that first shift. They cling to the mindset they grew up with, the mindset they see around them, the mindset that feels safe but keeps them poor. If you want a different result, you need a different way of thinking.

Scarcity vs. Abundance
The first and most important difference in mindset is the difference between scarcity and abundance.

Scarcity Thinking
Scarcity thinking says:

- There's never enough.
- Every dollar must be spent for survival.
- Money is something to consume, not something to grow.
- If someone else succeeds, it means less for me.

Scarcity makes you defensive. It keeps you living in fear. It convinces you that money is always about to run out, so you spend quickly before it disappears. Scarcity thinking pushes you to hoard when you should invest. It tricks you into grabbing money today instead of building for tomorrow.

Scarcity is why people blow their tax refunds on new furniture or gadgets instead of building an emergency fund. It's why people earning more than their parents still live paycheck to paycheck. It's why raises disappear the moment they arrive. Scarcity tells you that you'll never have enough, so you behave as if that were true.

Abundance Thinking

Abundance thinking says:

- There's enough if I manage it right.
- Money is a tool, not a trap.
- What I have can grow.
- Someone else's success does not take away mine.

Abundance isn't about luxury. It's not about pretending to be rich. It's about believing you can build more than what you have now. It's about making choices based on growth, not fear.

Abundance doesn't wait until everything is perfect to start. Abundance says, "I'll save something now, even if it's only a little." Abundance doesn't accept debt as a normal way of life. Abundance says, "Debt is a chain, and I refuse to wear it." Abundance doesn't excuse success as luck.

Abundance says, "Wealthy people think differently, and so can I."

The difference is small in words but massive in impact. Scarcity says, "I can't." Abundance says, "I will." Scarcity waits for permission. Abundance acts. Scarcity sees limits. Abundance sees opportunities.

This one shift changes everything. It's the line between living paycheck to paycheck forever and building wealth that lasts. Until you make this shift, every other financial strategy will fall apart. Once you do, every step forward builds faster and stronger.

How Scarcity Keeps You Poor

Scarcity isn't just a mindset you hold in your head. It shows up in the little choices you make every single day:

- You upgrade your phone on credit instead of waiting until you can actually afford it. You convince yourself it's "just $40 a month," but over two years you've chained yourself to a bill that drains money you could have saved or invested.

- You eat out four nights a week because cooking at home feels like deprivation. The truth is that convenience is costing you thousands every year. That money could have been buying freedom, but instead it bought short-term convenience.

- You fall for "buy now, pay later" because waiting feels impossible. A $200 splurge becomes four easy payments. Do it with ten different purchases at once and suddenly you're drowning in micro-debts that feel too small to notice individually but add up to a constant burden.

- You avoid investing because you think only the wealthy can start. You tell yourself you'll "begin later," not realizing that later costs you the one thing you can't replace: time.

Each decision feels small. Each feels harmless in the moment. But stacked together, they create a cycle that grinds people down:

1. **Spend.** You buy what makes you feel better right now.
2. **Borrow.** You swipe the card, take the loan, or click "pay later" when you run out of cash.
3. **Stress.** The bills pile up, the balances grow, and anxiety takes over.
4. **Repeat.** To escape the stress, you spend again, and the cycle starts over.

Scarcity locks you into this loop. It keeps you paycheck to paycheck, not because you don't earn money, but because you never create space. You never give your dollars the chance to work for you. Instead, you spend them the moment they arrive.

Living in survival mode feels normal to people trapped in scarcity. But survival mode never builds wealth. Survival mode is about today. Wealth is about tomorrow. If you stay in scarcity, you trade every tomorrow for a slightly more comfortable today and end up with nothing in the future.

The Trap of Instant Gratification

Modern life is built to sell you instant gratification. Companies spend billions on advertising making sure you want it now and figure out how to pay later. Every ad, every app, every checkout screen is engineered to push that button in your brain. "Buy today, zero down." "Split it into easy payments." "Treat yourself, you deserve it."

It's not by accident. It's by design.

The Psychology

Psychologists call it **delay discounting**. Humans naturally value rewards today more than rewards tomorrow. For example, If I offered someone $100 right now or $120 a year from now, most people would take the $100. Even though waiting gives you a guaranteed 20 percent return, the brain says, "I want it now."

Marketers know this. That's why stores place impulse buys at the register. That's why apps nudge you with one-click purchases. That's why streaming services auto-renew, subscription boxes auto-ship, and "limited-time offers" flood your inbox. They aren't just selling products. They're selling dopamine hits to a brain wired for "now."

For poor households, the temptation is even stronger. If you grew up in uncertainty, the mindset becomes, "Better spend it now before it disappears." That habit locks people into a cycle where money always disappears. The very thing that feels like security is the thing that ensures permanent instability.

The Cost

On the surface, instant gratification looks cheap. "Buy now, pay later" makes a $400 purchase feel painless. Four easy payments of $100. But miss one, and you face late fees. Stretch it longer, and interest turns your $400 item into $500 or more. That "easy" option just cost you a week of groceries.

Credit cards are no different. Put a $2,000 vacation on your card, pay the minimum balance, and by the time the interest runs its course, that trip actually ends up costing $5,000. You enjoyed the trip for seven days, but you pay for it for seven years.

The trap is subtle. Every time you say yes to instant gratification, you trade a small pleasure now for a bigger pain later. You buy the feeling of wealth without ever building actual wealth.

The Bigger Problem

Instant gratification doesn't just hurt your wallet. It rewires your habits. If every purchase is about what you can get today, you never build the patience required for long-term growth. You never experience the satisfaction of compounding. You never let your money breathe.

The reality is that most wealth is boring in the short term. It's putting money aside when no one's watching. It's saying no to the impulse buy so you can say yes to financial freedom later. It's training your brain to value future rewards more than temporary hits of pleasure.

Instant gratification feels like freedom, but it's slavery in disguise. It keeps you poor while convincing you that you're "treating yourself." It robs your future one swipe at a time. The wealthy learn to flip the script. They train themselves to wait, to invest, to build. That's how they buy freedom instead of payments.

The Wealth Mindset: Principles That Work

Abundance isn't just positive thinking. It's also practical thinking. Wealth mindset isn't about mantras or "manifesting." It's about building practical habits that put you in control. Here are three principles that separate the wealthy from the poor.

1. Pay Yourself First

Most people save "if there's anything left." There never is. Expenses expand until they consume the entire paycheck. That's why so many people with six-figure incomes still live paycheck to paycheck.

The wealthy pay themselves first. Before rent or mortgage. Before groceries. Before anything else, they set aside money for savings and investments. That way, building wealth isn't optional. It's automatic.

Research shows that people who automate savings build dramatically more wealth than those who wait until the end of the month.[27] The difference isn't income. It's the system used.

Even 10 percent of your paycheck adds up. If you net $60,000 a year, that's $6,000 saved each year. Invested at 7 percent, it can grow to over $560,000 in 30 years. That's without ever getting a raise. Increase your savings rate as income grows, and the numbers become life changing.

Practical tip: set up an automatic transfer on payday into a separate investment account. If you never see the money in your checking account, you won't spend it. Your future pays first. Your lifestyle adapts to what's left.

2. Think in Decades, Not Days

Poor thinking is short-term. "I just need to make it to Friday." That mindset survives the week but destroys the future.

Wealth thinking is long-term. "Where will this decision put me in 10 years?" Wealthy people aren't obsessed with instant results. They think in decades. They plan for compounding, for legacy, for systems that last.

Example: The $60,000 Car Decision

Imagine buying a brand new $60,000 car on credit. In 10 years, that car may only be worth $15,000. That's $45,000 gone, plus the thousands you paid in interest on the loan.

Now compare that to investing the same $60,000 in a broad index fund earning 7 percent annual growth:

- In 10 years, the same $60,000 could grow to about **$118,000**.
- In 20 years, it could grow to more than **$230,000**.
- In 30 years, it could grow to more than **$560,000**.

The income didn't change. The decision did. One choice left you with a depreciating asset and debt. The other left you with a growing asset that nearly quadruples in value over two decades, and if kept for another decade is worth almost 10 times the original investment.

This is how wealthy people think about every purchase. They don't just ask, "Can I afford it today?" They ask, "What will this cost me in future wealth if I buy it?" The poor look at today's price tag. The wealthy look at tomorrow's opportunity cost.

3. Use Money as a Tool

Poor thinking sees money as the end goal. "If I get more money, I'll finally be happy." But happiness isn't found in dollars. If that were true, lottery winners would stay wealthy, but most are completely broke within a few years.

Wealthy thinking sees money as a tool. A tool for freedom. A tool for opportunity. A tool for impact. Money itself isn't happiness, but it does create options. It lets you choose where you live, how you spend your time, and what kind of legacy you leave behind.

Once you see money as a tool, you stop wasting it on things that do nothing for you. Instead of draining money into car payments or gadgets that lose value over time, you put it toward assets that work for you. Instead of chasing status symbols, you buy freedom.

Money isn't the destination. It's the engine. And when you treat it as a tool, you stop being a servant to it and start making it serve you.

Stories of Mindset Shift
Maya's Story

Maya made $50,000 a year and lived paycheck to paycheck.

She believed she couldn't save until she made more. Then she shifted her mindset. She started by paying herself first, just $200 a month. At first it felt impossible. But one year later, she had $2,400 saved. That small change gave her confidence. Within five years, she had an emergency fund, started investing, and even took a modest vacation paid for in cash. The shift was not income. It was mindset.

Kevin's Story
Kevin earned six figures and always felt broke. He bought every new gadget, always leased luxury cars, and carried credit card balances every month. He lived in scarcity despite his income. When he shifted to long-term thinking, he stopped chasing luxuries and started investing. Ten years later, his net worth grew more than it had in the previous twenty.

Maria's Story
Maria grew up in a family where money was always scarce. She carried that thinking into adulthood. She believed investing was "too risky" and only for the rich. Her turning point came when she learned she could start with just $50 a month. That tiny start grew into $10,000 over several years. The amount mattered less than the shift: Maria went from fear to control.

Rewiring Your Mindset
Mindset shifts don't happen overnight. Years of habits and beliefs can't be erased in a single day. But change doesn't have to take decades either. The rewiring begins the moment you decide to think differently. Like any muscle, the more you practice, the stronger it gets. You can begin right now with three rewires.

Rewire #1: "I Pay Myself First"
Every paycheck, before bills, before rent or mortgage, before groceries, you save and invest. Even if it's only 5 percent, the act of paying yourself first builds the foundation of wealth. It proves to you that you come before creditors, before the landlord, before the supermarket.

When you put your future at the top of the list, everything else adapts. You'll find ways to live on what's left because people always do. But if you wait until the end of the month, nothing will ever be left.

Practical step: set up an automatic transfer the day your paycheck hits. Even if it's $50, do it now and do it consistently. That one decision rewires your brain to see saving as normal, not optional. Your future self will thank you.

Rewire #2: "I Think in Decades"
Most people think in days or weeks. "I just need to make it to Friday." Wealthy people think in decades. They ask, "Where will this decision put me in ten years?"

This one shift stops impulse purchases in their tracks. Before every major decision, pause and ask: Will this matter in ten years? Will this purchase make me wealthier or poorer over time?

Example: that $5,000 luxury vacation you're tempted to put on a credit card. In ten years, it'll just be a memory, but the debt could still be haunting you. Invest that same $5,000 instead, and in ten years it could be worth $10,000 or more.

Thinking in decades rewires your brain from consumer to builder. It teaches you to value compounding over comfort, growth over gratification.

Rewire #3: "Money Is My Tool"
Stop treating money as happiness. Start treating it as a resource. Happiness comes from meaning, relationships, and purpose. Money is the tool that gives you options to pursue those things without stress.

When you see money as a tool, you stop wasting it on status. You stop equating purchases with self-worth. Instead, you begin directing it toward freedom, growth, and impact.

A tool is something you control. When you understand that money is a tool, you stop being controlled by it.

Practical step: every time you spend, ask yourself, "What job is this dollar doing for me?" If the answer is "nothing," then you know you are misusing your tool.

Rewiring doesn't mean perfection. It means practice. Every time you choose to save before spending, think ten years ahead, or treat money as a tool, you strengthen new patterns. Over time, those rewires become your default. When your mindset changes, your bank account eventually follows.

Build Wealth in Your Head First
Scarcity thinking keeps you trapped. Abundance thinking sets you free. One mindset says there is never enough, so you spend and borrow until nothing is left. The other says there is enough to grow, so you save, invest, and create cushion. The results couldn't be more different.

Instant gratification steals your future. Delayed gratification multiplies it. One choice gives you a few minutes of pleasure. The other gives you decades of freedom. The poor keep trading tomorrow for today. The wealthy keep trading today for a better tomorrow.

If you want wealth in your bank account, start by building wealth in your head. Your thoughts drive your choices, and your choices build your habits. When you pay yourself first, you prove that your future matters more than temporary comfort. When you think long term, you stop wasting money on what disappears and start putting it toward what compounds. When you use money as a tool instead of a trophy, you build a life that works for you instead of a life that owns you.

The shift is simple, but it's not easy. It requires discipline in a world that screams at you to consume. It requires patience when everything around you promises speed and instant relief. It requires the courage to think differently than the people who stay stuck.

Change the way you think, and you change the way you live. Rewire your mind, and your bank account will follow. Build wealth in your head first, and eventually it'll show up everywhere else in your life.

7.
Cash Flow is King

Wealth starts with controlling what comes in and goes out. A real budget isn't restriction, it's freedom.

If mindset is the foundation of wealth, cash flow is the engine that makes everything move. Without control of your cash flow, wealth is impossible. You can have the best job in the world, the right mindset, and even well-performing investments, but if you don't control the movement of money in and out of your life, you'll stay stuck.

Cash flow is simply the movement of money: money in, money out. It's the income you earn, minus the bills you pay, minus the savings you keep, minus the investments you make. That flow is either working for you or against you.

If you control it, you build wealth. If you drift, you lose it. The scary part is that most people are drifting without realizing it. They assume that as long as they can cover their bills, they're "fine." But being fine is not the same as building wealth.

Most people think a budget is punishment. They imagine cutting back, depriving themselves, living like a monk, and saying no to every little pleasure. That's why budgeting feels scary. But the truth is the opposite. A budget isn't a restriction. It's direction. A budget is simply you telling your money where to go instead of wondering where it went.

This is the one rule that guarantees control: **Save at least half of what you make. Live on the other half.**

I call this the **Half Rule**, a system I developed to reset your financial life and force rapid progress.

The Half Rule
The Half Rule is simple, but it's radical compared to how most people live. Whatever you earn, you keep half. You can only use the

other half to cover housing, food, transportation, insurance, wants, and everything else.

If you earn $4,000 a month, you save $2,000. You live on $2,000.

If you earn $12,000 a month, you save $6,000. You live on $6,000.

If you earn $20,000 a month, you save $10,000. You live on $10,000.

The amounts change, but the ratio never does.

Why is this so powerful? Because if you save half, you guarantee stability. You guarantee discipline. You guarantee progress. No matter what your income level is, you're always building wealth. If you live on half, you create financial space where emergencies don't derail you, and opportunities don't pass you by.

Most people say, "That's impossible." But that's scarcity thinking. The truth is that most people waste half their money. They waste it on bigger cars, bigger houses, eating out, subscriptions they forgot about, gadgets that collect dust, and impulse purchases they regret the next morning. The Half Rule forces you to strip the waste and focus on what actually matters.

Living on half doesn't mean deprivation. It means intentionality. It means refusing to give every dollar away the moment it comes in. It means building the muscle of restraint so you can build the habit of wealth.

Why Half Works When Other Rules Fail
You've probably heard of the 50/30/20 rule or the 60/20/20 rule. They sound balanced. They make budgeting sound easier. But they also make savings optional. If your "20 percent savings" gets eaten up by lifestyle creep, you may convince yourself you are doing fine when you're not.

The Half Rule doesn't leave room for drift. It makes savings non-negotiable. It guarantees wealth because it puts building first and lifestyle second.

1. **It builds a cushion instantly.** Even on modest incomes, living on half builds an emergency fund fast. A few months in, you already have a cushion most people never see.

2. **It accelerates financial independence.** At a 50 percent savings rate, you can retire in about 15 years. That isn't theory. That's math. No matter your income, if you live on half, financial freedom comes fast.

3. **It kills lifestyle creep.** Every raise, every bonus, every side hustle – half is automatically saved. Your lifestyle never outruns your income. You rise faster than your expenses.

4. **It forces creativity.** Living on half makes you sharper with expenses. You negotiate harder. You cut the fat. You find smarter ways to solve problems. You thrive because your brain is trained to find value instead of chasing status.

Every other budgeting method tries to balance categories. The Half Rule creates wealth as the first priority. Once you do that, everything else adjusts around it.

The Psychology of Half
Why do people resist saving half? It usually comes down to three things: confusion, belief, and fear.

- **They confuse wants with needs.** A luxury car feels like a need. It's not. A $1,000 phone upgrade feels like a need. It's not. Needs are food, shelter, and safety. Everything else is negotiable.

- **They believe half is impossible.** They tell themselves their situation is different. But half is always possible if you build toward it. Start at 10 percent. Move to 20. Then 30. Then 50. Progress is the path.

- **They fear sacrifice.** They think living on half means misery, empty fun, and a boring life. The truth is, living on half means clarity. You stop stressing about money because you finally control it. Most people who adopt the Half Rule discover they enjoy life more because they no longer live under constant financial pressure.

Psychologically, the Half Rule is powerful because it flips the script. Instead of thinking, "I can't afford to save," you start thinking, "I can't afford not to." Once that shift happens, the rule becomes liberating, not limiting.

Examples at Different Income Levels
(assuming an annual return of 7 percent on invested savings)

$40,000 Income
Take-home: about $3,200 per month.
Half Rule: $1,600 savings, $1,600 expenses.

It's tight, but possible. It forces discipline with housing and transportation. It may mean roommates, a modest car, cooking at home, and no frivolous subscriptions. But the payoff is huge: $20,000 saved in just over a year. That's more than most people making $40,000 ever save in a decade.

$80,000 Income
Take-home: about $5,300 per month.
Half Rule: $2,650 savings, $2,650 expenses.

This level allows comfortable housing, transportation, and some lifestyle flexibility. But the real power is in the savings. $32,000 a year stacks quickly. In 10 years, invested with growth, that could become more than $500,000. Most people with $80,000 incomes are still poor after a decade. With the Half Rule, you are halfway to millionaire status.

$150,000 Income
Take-home: about $9,500 per month.
Half Rule: $4,750 savings, $4,750 expenses.

Plenty of room for a nice lifestyle while still saving nearly $60,000 a year. In 15 years, you have more than $1.5 million invested. By your 40s or 50s, you are financially independent while your peers are still buried in mortgage debt and car payments.

$250,000 Income
Take-home: about $15,500 per month.
Half Rule: $7,750 savings, $7,750 expenses.

This is how wealthy people build wealth fast. Over $90,000 a year saved, $1.3 million in 10 years, and more than $3.5 million in 20 years. This is why many high earners either end up rich or end up poor. The Half Rule is the dividing line.

Step-by-Step to the Half Rule
Not everyone can flip a switch and save 50 percent immediately. That's fine. The Half Rule is not about perfection. It is about progress. You build towards it over time.

1. **Start with 10 percent.** Automate savings before anything else. If you're at zero, get to 10. That single habit changes everything.

2. **Cut obvious waste.** Dining out, subscriptions, unnecessary shopping. Frees up $500–$1,000 a month easily. Most households waste at least this much without even realizing it.

3. **Upgrade slowly.** Every raise? Save half. Every bonus? Save half. Every side hustle? Save half. That way, lifestyle never outruns income.

4. **Work toward 30 percent.** Within a year or two, you can hit 30 percent by trimming the fat. Once you're at 30, momentum builds fast.

5. **Push to 50 percent.** As income rises, half becomes natural. At first, it feels extreme. Eventually, it feels normal.

The Half Rule is a journey. But the principle is always the same – half is yours to keep. If you keep half, you'll never be poor again. The person who always saves half may not drive the fanciest car in the neighborhood, but they'll be the one who retires free while the neighbors are still making payments.

A Month-by-Month Half Budget Transformation

Let's walk through a real case study of how someone goes from poor to fully following the Half Rule within one year.

Case Study: Maya

Income: $50,000 salary
Take-home pay: about $3,300 a month

- **Month 1:** Maya starts with awareness. She writes down every expense for 30 days. The numbers surprise her. $500 on dining out. $200 in random subscriptions she barely uses. $300 in impulse shopping from late-night online orders. At the end of the month, she has no savings. Her money came in, her money went out, and she could now explain where most of it went.

- **Month 2:** Maya makes her first big shift. She sets up an automatic transfer of $500 to a savings account on payday. She cancels the subscriptions and cuts dining in half by meal prepping twice a week. At the end of the month, she has $1,000 saved for the first time in her life. She feels a spark of control.

- **Month 3:** Maya moves to zero-based budgeting. Every dollar she earns gets an assignment before the month begins. She trims her lifestyle even further and calls her insurance company to negotiate her car and renter's premiums. Her bills drop by $75 a month. Savings rise to $1,000 a month.

- **Month 6:** Maya has $6,000 saved and has paid off $1,500 in old credit card debt. Her emergency fund is almost funded. For the first time in years, she can handle a surprise car repair without panic. She notices her stress level dropping and her confidence rising.

- **Month 12:** Maya now saves $1,600 every month while living on $1,700. She has $19,000 saved, no credit card debt, and a system that feels normal instead of extreme. She is fully following the Half Rule.

Fast Forward Ten Years Later: Same job. Same income. But different result. By saving $1,600 a month and investing it at 7 percent growth, Maya has over $275,000. She went from drifting paycheck to paycheck to building real freedom. All because she chose to live by the Half Rule.

The Math of Half
The Half Rule is powerful because the math behind it is undeniable. At a 50 percent savings rate, you can retire in about 15 years. That isn't a motivational slogan. It's simple arithmetic.

Here's why:
- Save half and invest at 7 percent annual growth.

- In 15 years, you'll have built up savings equal to 15 years of expenses.

- At that point, your investments generate income that can cover your lifestyle.

Now compare savings rates:
- At a **10 percent savings rate**, it takes about 50 years to reach financial independence. That's why most people retire at 65 or 70.

- At a **20 percent savings rate**, it takes about 35 years. You can retire a decade earlier than most, but it's still a long grind.

- At a **50 percent savings rate**, it takes just 15 years. The Half Rule compresses decades into years.

This is the wealth shortcut most people overlook. They're trying to out-earn their expenses, but you can't out-earn bad habits. The Half Rule changes the game. You don't just earn more. You keep more. Keeping is what creates freedom.

Stories of People Who Shifted

Numbers are powerful, but stories make them real. Here are three examples of people who adopted the Half Rule and changed their lives.

Maya – The Builder

Maya earned $50,000 a year as an office professional and lived paycheck to paycheck. At first, the idea of saving half felt impossible. She started small, but after taking a hard look at her expenses and making changes, she was saving half of her income automatically after one year. Before turning 35, she had $120,000 invested and a system that ran itself. While her friends joked about being "broke adults," Maya quietly built the foundation for financial freedom.

Ten-Year Projection: If she continues investing $1,600 a month at 7 percent, she'll have over $275,000 in ten years, and more than $750,000 in twenty.

James – The Business Owner

James owned a small contracting business and earned six figures, but he always felt broke. The house, the truck, and the vacations looked successful, but his finances told another story. At 40, he decided to take control. He applied the Half Rule, reduced his spending, and redirected the difference into investments and business expansion. Within twelve years, his net worth grew to more than $1 million while he still lived comfortably. His peers will work into their 60s. James can choose whether he wants to or not.

Ten-Year Projection: Maintaining a $4,000 monthly investment at 7 percent growth builds roughly $690,000. After twenty years, more than $1.9 million.

Maria – The Cycle Breaker

Maria worked as a nurse and raised two children on her own. She believed saving half was impossible. Still, she began with $200 a month, consistent and automatic. Every time her income increased, she raised her savings rate. By her late 30s, she was saving half of her paycheck and teaching her kids how money really works. Maria may not be a millionaire yet, but she now has financial security and peace of mind. She ended the cycle of stress and scarcity that defined her childhood and replaced it with stability and purpose.

Ten-Year Projection: At her current savings rate, she will surpass $250,000 in invested assets before age 45, creating a lasting foundation for her family.

These stories show the same truth: income level is not the deciding factor. Mindset and discipline are. The Half Rule works for a teacher, an executive, and even someone who grew up in poverty. The principle is universal.

The Safety Net: Why You Need an Emergency Fund

Cash flow isn't only about budgeting and saving. It's also about protecting yourself from the unexpected. Life will always test your systems. If you don't have an emergency fund, you're one crisis away from falling back into debt.

An emergency fund isn't optional. It's your safety net. It keeps you from swiping a credit card when the car breaks down, when the roof leaks, when your child needs medical care, or when you lose a big client. Without it, all of your wealth systems collapse the first time life punches you in the face.

Think of it this way… Building wealth without an emergency fund is like building a house with no insurance. It looks fine until the storm hits. Then everything you worked for gets wiped away.

How Much Do You Need?
The size of your emergency fund depends on how you earn your income. Not all jobs or businesses carry the same level of risk.

For Salaried Employees
If you earn a steady paycheck, your risk is generally lower. You should have at least **three months of living expenses** saved in cash. This means covering your true essentials: housing, utilities, food, insurance, transportation, and anything else required to keep your household running. With three months in the bank, you can survive a layoff, medical leave, or a surprise repair without panic.

For Commission-Based Workers and Business Owners
If your income depends on sales, commissions, or your own business, your risk is much higher. You don't have the guarantee of a steady paycheck. You need more of a cushion. Your emergency fund should be **six to twelve months of living expenses.**

This may sound extreme, but it's reality. Businesses have slow times and often fail. Commissions dry up. Markets slow down. A twelve-month cushion allows you to make smart, patient decisions instead of desperate ones. It keeps you from selling investments at the worst time or taking out predatory loans just to survive.

Where to Keep It
Your emergency fund should sit in a **high-yield savings account** or a **money market account.** It should be liquid and accessible, but separate from your regular spending account.

Don't invest it in stocks. Don't chase returns. This money is about stability, not growth. If it earns a few percent in interest, great. But the goal isn't to grow. The goal is to be there the moment you need it.

Build It First

Before you go deep into investing, before you take on risk, build your emergency fund. Without it, one unexpected event can wipe out years of progress.

An emergency fund isn't exciting. It won't make you rich. It won't impress your friends. But it will keep you from being poor when life gets hard. That makes it one of the most powerful financial tools you'll ever own.

Action Plan: Build Your Half Budget

Cash flow is king. If you don't control what comes in and what goes out, you'll never build wealth. You'll always be reacting instead of leading.

The Half Rule makes it simple. Save at least half of what you make. Live on the rest. No gimmicks, no categories, no complicated formulas. Just half. It's straightforward enough for anyone to understand, but strong enough to build generational wealth.

Your challenge:
1. Write down your monthly income.

2. Cut it in half.

3. Commit to saving and investing that half.

4. Adjust your lifestyle to fit the other half.

At first, it'll feel impossible. Then it'll feel uncomfortable. Later on, it'll feel normal. Once it becomes normal, wealth builds faster than you ever thought possible.

This single choice separates you from 99 percent of people. It guarantees stability. It guarantees progress. Most of all, it guarantees freedom.

Cash flow is king. Master it, and you master money.

8.

Kill the Bad Debt, Build Good Credit

Not all debt is created equal. Learn how to destroy the bad, rebuild the good, and use credit as a tool instead of a crutch.

Debt is the great pretender. It looks like help. It feels like progress. But most of the time, it's chains.

Here's the brutal truth… Any debt that doesn't buy an income-producing asset is **bad debt**.

If the money you borrow does not generate more money than it costs, it's toxic. Period.

That means the things most people never question – cars, phones, even primary residences – aren't investments. They're liabilities dressed up as assets. They may feel like signs of success, but in reality they're silent drains that rob you of your future.

What Counts as Bad Debt

Bad debt is simple; it takes money out of your pocket every month without ever putting money back. It feels normal because everyone does it, but "normal" is the problem. Normal is poor.

- **Cars.** A car begins losing value the second you drive it off the lot. Five years later, it may be worth half (or less) of what you paid for it. Finance it with interest, and the total cost is thousands higher than the sticker price. You're literally paying extra for something that becomes worth less every day.

- **Phones.** That $1,200 smartphone on a financing plan drains your cash flow for something that'll be outdated in two years. Add in the interest or "upgrade every year" cycle, and you never own anything outright. It's just an endless drain dressed up as convenience.

- **Primary residences.** This one shocks people. A house feels like an investment, but if it doesn't produce rental income, it's a liability. Taxes, insurance, maintenance, and mortgage interest all drain you every month. Even if it goes up in value on paper, it's still taking money from you, not putting money in your pocket.

- **Credit cards.** With average APRs over 20 percent, they're wealth killers. Carry a balance, and you're handing over future freedom in exchange for short-term spending.

- **Student loans.** Education can be valuable, but not all degrees are worth the debt. Borrowing six figures for a degree that produces no income is financial self-sabotage. If the cost of education doesn't match the career payoff, it's bad debt.

- **Personal loans for consumption.** Financing furniture, vacations, or shopping trips doesn't create value. It only creates chains.

Simply put, if what you're buying with debt doesn't produce income, it's bad debt. If it's not putting money in your pocket, it's pulling money out.

Good Debt Defined

There's only one kind of debt that earns the label "good": business or investment debt that creates positive cash flow. Good debt isn't about appearances. It's about multiplication.

- **Rental property mortgages.** A mortgage on a property that earns more in rent than it costs in mortgage, taxes, and maintenance is good debt. The property pays for itself and produces profit.

- **Business term loans or SBA loans.** Borrowing to acquire or start a business that generates reliable income is a productive use of debt. When structured correctly, these loans create assets that outlive the repayment schedule and produce long-term equity.

- **Business lines of credit.** Borrowing to buy inventory that sells at a profit multiplies your money. The cost of borrowing is outweighed by the revenue you generate.

- **Equipment loans.** If financing equipment allows a business to expand, produce more, and increase revenue, that debt is productive. It pays for itself and creates additional cash flow.

Good debt multiplies your income. Bad debt multiplies your stress.

Why Bad Debt Is So Dangerous
Bad debt destroys wealth in two ways, and both are brutal.

1. **Cash flow drain.** Monthly payments rob you of the cushion that creates freedom. You work for lenders instead of yourself. Every payment to the bank is money you can no longer invest, save, or use to create options. You become trapped in a cycle where the lender profits and you stay stuck.

2. **Lost compounding.** Every dollar that goes to interest is a dollar that could have been invested. The longer you pay lenders, the more wealth you forfeit. Over decades, the lost opportunity compounds into hundreds of thousands of dollars in missed growth.

Example: A $40,000 car loan at 7 percent isn't just a car. It's 60 months of servitude. By the time it's paid off, you have a car worth maybe $20,000 at best and have also handed thousands to the bank in interest. Compare that to investing the same money, and the opportunity cost is staggering.

Your "dream home"? If it costs $3,000 a month and produces no rental income, it's not an investment. It's an expense. Even if it appreciates in value, that doesn't make it an asset in your favor. Appreciation on paper doesn't erase the years of taxes, repairs, interest, and insurance draining you along the way. You'll also always need somewhere to live, so you can't just sell it and take the profits without having to find another house.

Before and After: The Debt Trap vs. Financial Freedom
Before: Living the Normal Way

Take Daniel. He earns $80,000 a year, which is about $5,300 per month after taxes. By all appearances, he's "doing fine." He drives a $40,000 sedan on a five-year loan, which costs him $650 a month. His phone plan is $80, but he finances his $1,200 phone for another $50 monthly. His mortgage payment on a $350,000 house runs $2,100 a month, not including taxes and insurance. Add $400 in credit card minimums, plus student loan payments, dining out, and entertainment, and Daniel's cash flow disappears before the month even ends.

Daniel isn't poor in appearance. He lives in a nice house, drives a nice car, and posts vacation photos online. But financially, he's drowning. His net worth is near zero. His emergency fund is nonexistent. He's one job loss away from disaster.

After: Living the Wealth Way

Now imagine the same Daniel with the same income, but a different mindset. Instead of a new $40,000 sedan, he drives a reliable $12,000 used car bought in cash. His phone is an older model he owns outright, not financed. Instead of stretching for a "dream house," he rents a modest apartment for $1,200 while saving for income-producing real estate later.

With these choices, Daniel follows the Half Rule. He saves $2,600 every month while living on the other $2,600. Within one year, he has over $30,000 in savings. In five years, he has nearly $200,000 invested and compounding. He's building wealth, not appearances.

The Difference

Both Daniels earn the same salary. Both have access to the same opportunities. One chooses debt, the other chooses discipline. After ten years, the "normal" Daniel still owes thousands on depreciating assets, while the wealth-focused Daniel owns assets that produce income and a portfolio that works for him.

Your financial future doesn't depend on your income level nearly as much as it depends on how you use debt. Avoid bad debt, and your cash flow becomes your engine. Take on bad debt, and your cash flow becomes your prison.

The Psychology of Debt

Bad debt thrives because it preys on human emotion. Lenders don't just sell loans. They sell feelings.

- **Status.** A luxury car makes you feel successful. The debt makes the feeling possible long before the reality is there.

- **Convenience.** A financed phone plan makes the newest gadget feel affordable. Instead of waiting or saving, you swipe the card today and pay for months.

- **Security.** A big house feels like safety. But the mortgage payment, property taxes, and repairs can turn that feeling of security into the source of your greatest stress.

Debt sells you a feeling today while stealing your future tomorrow.

This is why Americans collectively hold over $1 trillion in credit card debt.[31] The system is designed to normalize it. Credit card offers arrive in the mail. Car ads scream "low monthly payment." Student loans are marketed as "good debt." The messaging is relentless. But here's the truth: **normal is poor.**

Case Study: The Forever Home Trap vs. The Freedom Plan
The Trap

Lisa was 32 and earning around $120,000 a year as a successful realtor. Like many in her field, she believed homeownership was the ultimate badge of success. She stretched to buy a $500,000 "forever home," convinced it would be her best investment. Her mortgage, taxes, and insurance totaled $3,800 per month, consuming more than half of her take-home pay. On paper, she owned a beautiful home. In reality, the home owned her. Vacations went on credit cards. Her emergency fund never grew beyond $2,000. When the roof needed replacing, she took out a home equity loan. The house that was supposed to build wealth quietly drained it instead.

The Plan

Maya, the same age and earning a similar income with her partner, made a different choice. Instead of buying the biggest home they could afford, they rented a $1,600 apartment and lived well within their means. They followed the Half Rule and invested $3,000 every month. Within three years, they had saved over $100,000. By year five, their investments totaled more than $200,000. They used part of that money for a down payment on a duplex, where the rent from one unit covered most of the mortgage. Five years later, they owned two additional rental properties and had built a net worth exceeding $500,000.

The Lesson

Lisa believed her home was an investment, but it became a liability that limited her freedom. Maya delayed gratification, built savings, and turned her money into assets that paid her back. Both earned similar incomes. The difference was discipline and perspective. One bought image. The other built independence.

The Plan to Fix Bad Debt

You can't wish debt away. You can't manifest it gone. You need a plan. A step-by-step system that turns your money back into a weapon for you, instead of a weapon against you.

Step 1: List Every Debt

You can't defeat what you refuse to see. Most people avoid looking at their balances because it feels painful. That avoidance is why they stay stuck.

Sit down with a pen and paper or a spreadsheet. Write down:

- Every balance.
- Every interest rate.
- Every minimum payment.
- Every due date.

Add it up. See the real number. You may feel overwhelmed, but this is where control begins. A problem you face gets solved. A problem you avoid gets worse.

Step 2: Attack Toxic Payments
Phones, cars, homes… These are the "normal" debts that chain people to the middle class. They feel acceptable because "everyone does it." But if everyone around you is poor, do you want to do what everyone else does?

Phones:
- Stop financing phones. Buy used or last year's model in cash. It works the same and costs a fraction.

- If you must finance, attack the balance aggressively. Don't let a $40 per month plan turn into a lifestyle trap for decades.

- Example: A $1,200 iPhone on payments bleeds out much more than a $300 phone bought outright. Over 10 years, that difference can mean tens of thousands invested or wasted.

Cars:
- Never lease. Leasing is renting with interest and zero ownership at the end. Plus it can be incredibly expensive to get out early if something changes in your life.

- Never finance luxury. If you can't pay cash, you can't afford it.

- If financing is absolutely necessary, buy modest, reliable, and drive it for 10 years or longer. That alone saves hundreds of thousands over a lifetime.

Homes:

- Don't let the bank tell you what you can "afford." The bank's approval protects them, not you.

- If you already own, minimize costs. Refinance wisely when rates drop, but don't use your equity as an ATM.

- Consider house hacking. Rent a room, a basement, or an accessory dwelling. Turn a liability into an income-producing asset.

Step 3: Choose Your Attack Method

Once you have the list, you need a strategy. There are two proven methods:

- **Debt Snowball:** Pay off the smallest balances first. You build momentum fast and feel the progress.

- **Debt Avalanche:** Pay off the highest interest first. You save the most money mathematically.

Both work. The only wrong choice is doing nothing. Pick one and commit.

Step 4: Reinvest the Freed Cash Flow

The most dangerous mistake is paying off debt and then letting lifestyle creep eat up the freed money. Every time you kill a payment, redirect that money into savings and investments. This is how you turn pain into progress. If your car payment disappears, but you immediately upgrade your lifestyle, you've learned nothing.

Special Category: Student Loans

Student loans deserve their own spotlight because they trap millions of Americans in quiet financial prisons. They're sold as the "good debt" that always pays off, but the reality is much messier. Some degrees absolutely do lead to higher lifetime earnings. Many do not. A degree in medicine, law, or engineering can open doors to salaries that far exceed the cost of the loan. A degree that doesn't translate into higher income becomes a lifelong burden.

Unlike other forms of borrowing, student loans are sticky. You can't walk away from them like a leased car. You can't discharge most of them in bankruptcy. Once you sign, they're yours until you pay them, refinance them, or qualify for forgiveness programs. That permanence is what makes them so dangerous.

How to Calculate ROI (Return on Investment) on a Degree

You should treat an education decision the same way you would treat an investment in a business. What's the cost, and what's the expected return?

Here's a simple way to calculate it:

1. **Find the Total Cost of Education**
   Add up tuition, fees, books, and living expenses. If you're borrowing, include the interest you'll likely pay as well.

   Example: A four-year program costs $25,000 per year = $100,000 total. At 6 percent interest, if you repay over 10 years, the true cost is closer to $135,000.

2. **Estimate Your Expected Income**
   Look up realistic salaries for your degree field. Don't ever use "best case" numbers. Use median salaries reported by Bureau of Labor Statistics or industry data. Make sure those figures are in the state you live in, or plan to work in.

   Example: The median salary for a new social worker is about $55,000. The median salary for a new registered nurse is about $77,000.

3. **Subtract Alternative Income**
   Ask yourself: what could you earn without the degree? If you could earn $40,000 without it and $55,000 with it, your "degree boost" is only $15,000 per year.

4. **Calculate the Payback Period**
   Divide the true loan cost by the degree boost.

   Example: $135,000 ÷ $15,000 = 9 years just to break even.

5. **Decide If It's Worth It**
   If the payback period is under 5 to 7 years, the loan may be reasonable. If it stretches into decades, you are chaining yourself to debt that will hold you back.

This ROI test changes everything. It shows you whether the degree is a wealth-building asset or just an expensive liability.

How to Handle Student Loans
Manageable Balances
If your balance can be killed in five years or less, go all in. Cut luxuries, funnel every extra dollar into payments, and be done with it. Five years of sacrifice beats 30 years of minimum payments.

Overwhelming Balances
If your balance is massive, you need a dual strategy: raise your income and cut your lifestyle. Take extra shifts, pursue promotions, start a side business, or even move to a city where salaries are higher in your field. Every extra dollar you can throw at the loan shortens the timeline.

Forgiveness and Programs
If you qualify for programs like Public Service Loan Forgiveness (PSLF) or income-driven repayment, use them. But never plan your future around them. They change with politics, paperwork gets messy, and promises are not always delivered. If it happens, great. If it doesn't, you still need a plan to win on your own.

The Emotional Trap
Student loans also carry shame. Many borrowers regret taking them or feel tricked into signing without understanding the cost. That shame leads to avoidance. Payments become background noise, and

the balance hardly moves. Ignoring the debt doesn't make it smaller. It only makes the interest grow.

You need to separate your emotions from the numbers. Student debt isn't a moral failure. It's a financial challenge. Just like every financial challenge, it can be solved with a plan.

Case Example: Maya's Two Paths
Maya graduates with $80,000 in student loans at 6 percent interest. She earns $50,000 a year.

- **Path 1: Minimum Payments**
  Maya pays $500 a month, the minimum. After 10 years, she has paid $60,000 but still owes $45,000. The debt feels endless.

- **Path 2: Aggressive Attack**
  Maya lives lean, pays $1,500 a month, and is debt-free in five years. Total interest paid is $12,000. At 30 years old, she has her freedom back.

Both Mayas start the same. One is in debt well into her 40s. One is free before 30. The difference is urgency and discipline.

The Long-Term Cost
Student loans not only take your money each month. They steal your future growth.

Imagine you pay $500 per month for 20 years. That's $120,000 out of pocket. If that money had been invested at 7 percent, it would have grown to about $250,000. The true cost of your education isn't just $120,000. It's over $370,000 when you include the opportunity cost of lost compounding.

The Bottom Line
Education can be a powerful wealth-builder. But you have to measure it like an investor. If the loan cost exceeds the value of the income stream, it's toxic and must be eliminated quickly (or never

taken in the first place). Use the ROI test before borrowing. If you already have the loans, face them directly and build a plan to escape.

Your education should be an asset, not a lifelong liability.

Building Credit the Right Way

Not all debt is evil. Credit itself is neutral. It's simply a tool. The way you use it decides whether it makes you stronger or destroys you. Strong credit doesn't mean carrying balances or juggling cards. It means proving to the financial system that you are responsible, and that you can be trusted with money.

Good credit unlocks lower interest rates, cheaper insurance, higher paying jobs, and better access to business or real estate loans. Bad credit costs you thousands in extra payments and often blocks you from opportunities altogether.

Why Credit Matters

Credit scores affect more than loans. Employers sometimes check them when hiring. Landlords look at them before renting. Insurance companies use them when setting rates. A strong score signals that you follow through, while a weak score tells the world you're a risk.

You don't need perfect credit. But you do need solid, consistent credit that keeps doors open.

How Credit Scores Work

Your credit score is made up of five weighted parts:

1. **Payment History (35%)** – Paying on time is the single biggest factor. One missed payment can haunt you for years. Defaults are catastrophic.

2. **Credit Utilization (30%)** – How much of your available credit you actually use. Under 30 percent utilization is okay. Under 10 percent is excellent.

3. **Length of History (15%)** – The longer your accounts stay open and active, the stronger your score.

4. **Credit Mix (10%)** – Lenders like to see variety: a credit card, a personal loan, a mortgage.

5. **New Credit (10%)** – Too many applications in a short time lower your score temporarily.

Understanding this breakdown helps you play the game strategically.

Safe Tools to Build Credit
1. Credit Card
- Use just one card if you are starting out.

- Keep utilization under 10 percent. If your limit is $2,000, don't let your balance go above $200.

- Pay it in full every month automatically. Never carry a balance for the sake of "building credit." That's a myth.

2. Small Personal Loan
- Borrow $500 to $1,000. Pay it off in six months.

- The loan is small enough that you can handle it, but it builds history and shows you can manage installment debt.

3. Credit Builder Loan
- Many credit unions and online banks offer these. You make payments into a savings account you get back at the end.

- It's like training wheels for credit: safe, structured, and risk-free.

4. Authorized User
- If you have a trusted family member with excellent credit, ask to be added as an authorized user.

- Their history gets added to your report, boosting your score quickly.

- Caution: make sure this person manages credit responsibly. If they miss payments, it will hurt you too.

Common Credit Myths That Keep People Stuck

- **"You need to carry a balance to build credit."** False. Carrying a balance only builds interest for the bank, not your score. Paying in full shows responsibility.

- **"Many cards build better credit."** False. More accounts can help, but only if managed well. One card used wisely is stronger than five cards used recklessly.

- **"Closing old accounts helps clean things up."** False. Closing old accounts often hurts because it shortens your credit history. Keep them open if possible.

- **"Checking your credit lowers your score."** False. Checking your own score is considered a soft inquiry. Only hard inquiries from lenders affect it.

The Right Mindset

Building credit isn't about borrowing money you can't afford. It's about proving to the system that you could borrow but choose not to abuse it. Lenders don't reward people who stay perpetually in debt. They reward people who show control.

Think of credit like a report card. You don't get an "A" by turning in sloppy work. You get an "A" by showing you can be trusted to do what's expected, consistently.

Practical Steps to Build or Rebuild Credit

1. **Start with one secured card.** Deposit $200–$500, use it lightly, pay in full. This builds a track record.

2. **Add a small installment loan.** This balances your "credit mix." Pay it off quickly.

3. **Keep balances low.** Never let utilization climb above 10 percent. Set alerts if you need to.

4. **Never miss a payment.** Automate minimums to protect yourself from mistakes.

5. **Let accounts age.** Keep your oldest accounts open as long as possible.

6. **Check your report.** Review your credit report annually at AnnualCreditReport.com and dispute errors.

Case Example: James Rebuilds His Score

James had poor credit after years of occasional missed payments due to challenges with his business start-up. His score was 580. He started with a $500 secured card, charged $50 per month, and paid it in full. Six months later, he took out a $1,000 personal loan, paid it off in six months, and added an authorized user account with his father's long-standing card. Within two years, his score rose to 720. That jump saved him thousands when he eventually financed a business loan at 6 percent instead of 12 percent.

The Payoff of Good Credit

Strong credit isn't about bragging rights. It's about freedom. A high score means:

- Lower mortgage payments.
- Lower insurance premiums.
- Better terms on business loans.
- Less stress when renting or applying for opportunities.

Good credit isn't the same as wealth, but it is a multiplier. It makes wealth-building cheaper, faster, and smoother. Bad credit does the opposite.

The Future Cost of Debt
Debt doesn't just hurt you today. It robs your future self. Every monthly payment you make is not just money leaving your account. It's compounding growth you will never see.

Here's the math:
- $1,000 invested monthly at 7 percent = **$120,000 in 10 years**.
- $1,000 invested monthly at 7 percent = **$260,000 in 20 years**.
- $1,000 invested monthly at 7 percent = **$500,000 in 30 years**.

So when you hand $1,000 to a lender each month, you aren't just paying them today. You're taking half a million dollars away from your future self, thirty years from now.

That's the hidden cost most people never see. They think about the car payment or the phone payment in isolation. They never think about the lost compounding. But lost compounding is what keeps people poor.

Bad debt isn't just an expense. It's a time thief. It steals decades of growth from you and hands it to someone else.

The Debt Elimination Roadmap
Killing bad debt feels as overwhelming as a climber would if they stared at the whole mountain. The balances look huge, the interest feels endless, and you start believing it'll take forever. That mindset keeps people stuck. The way out is to break it into stages. Focus on one layer at a time, stack small wins, and roll the momentum forward. Three years is enough time to completely transform your financial picture if you attack it with discipline.

Stage 1: First 0–12 Months
Target: The smallest and fastest-kill debts.
Your first year is about building quick wins. You need the psychological boost of seeing debts disappear, and you need to free up cash flow that will later become your snowball.

- **Phones.** If you're financing a phone, pay it off and stop upgrading every cycle. Buy used or last year's model in cash going forward. This alone can free up $40–$60 a month.

- **Credit cards.** Knock out balances under $2,000. These are the chains that feel small but cost you huge interest every month. Use the snowball method for momentum.

- **Credit building.** Open a secured credit card or take out a small personal loan ($500–$1,000) and pay it back quickly. This begins rewriting your credit history in a positive direction.

- **Lifestyle leaks.** Cancel the streaming services you never watch. Cook more meals at home. Negotiate your phone bill. Free up $200–$500 a month and throw it directly at debt.

Result: Within a year, you've eliminated quick-hit debts, freed up meaningful monthly cash, and started laying the foundation for a stronger credit score. That momentum sets the tone for everything else.

Stage 2: 12–24 Months
Target: Larger recurring payments.
Now you turn your attention to the big monthly drains that keep most people trapped.

- **Car loans.** Sell overpriced vehicles. If you're driving a shiny new $60,000 SUV with a $900 payment, it's time to get real. Buy a reliable brand used car in cash, even if it's not flashy. Redirect that payment every month into savings and investments. Over time, that choice alone creates six figures in additional wealth.

- **Student loans.** If your balance is under $25,000, kill it aggressively in this stage. If your balance is larger, target the high-interest portions while keeping minimums on the rest.

Refinancing to a lower rate may help, but only if it shortens the payoff window.

- **Personal loans.** Pay off high-interest personal loans or refinance them at lower rates if possible. Don't let them drag on.

- **Credit building, round two.** Add another safe tool, like a credit-builder loan from a credit union or get added as an authorized user on a responsible family member's card. The goal is to show consistent on-time payments and low utilization.

Result: By the end of year two, your largest recurring drains are either gone or shrinking fast, and your credit score is climbing steadily. Your freed-up cash flow is no longer hundreds… It's in the thousands.

Stage 3: 24–36 Months
Target: Long-term traps.
This stage is where you take on the structural changes that make the biggest long-term difference.

- **Primary residence.** If your home is draining you, take action. Options: refinance into a shorter term to kill the mortgage faster, downsize to a more affordable home, or house hack by renting out a room, basement, or accessory unit. A house is only an asset if it generates cash flow. Don't ever refinance just to lower the payment. This only makes your mortgage last longer and you'll usually end up paying more in interest throughout the life of the loan.

- **Snowballing.** Continue rolling your freed cash into remaining debts. If student loans remain, they are now the focus. If you still have lingering credit card balances, crush them completely.

- **Leveraging strong credit.** By this point, your score should be significantly higher. That opens the door to loans that can be used strategically – for a business, for a rental property, or for another income-producing investment.

- **Half Rule integration.** Automate half of your newly freed cash flow into savings and investments. If you free up $2,000 a month, $1,000 goes directly into building wealth. This locks in progress and prevents lifestyle creep from stealing your wins.

Result: After three years, your toxic debts are either gone or fully under control. Your credit score is strong enough to open opportunities instead of closing them, and your cash flow is freed up to build wealth instead of feeding lenders.

Quick Reference: What to Kill First
Debt elimination isn't random. Attack in this order:

1. Phones and small balances (easy kills, quick wins).
2. Credit cards under $5,000 (high interest, fast compounding).
3. Car loans (huge monthly drain, no return on investment).
4. Student loans (long-term anchor, eliminate aggressively once smaller debts are gone).
5. Primary residence restructuring (fix the big trap last).

Action Plan: Kill Bad Debt, Build Credit the Right Way
Bad debt is poison. It feels normal because everyone around you carries it. But normal is poor.

Cars, phones, primary homes, credit cards, student loans – unless they generate income, they are toxic.

The plan is simple but powerful:

1. Write down every debt. Face it.

2. Attack the toxic ones first. Stack quick wins.
3. Reinvest every freed-up dollar into savings and investments.
4. Build credit with small, intentional tools. Not reckless borrowing.

When you kill bad debt, you free your cash flow. When you free your cash flow, you create wealth.

Debt elimination is not about deprivation. It's about transformation. Every payment you kill is a raise you give yourself. Every dollar you redirect is a step toward freedom.

Your Next Step: Apply the Roadmap
Reading about debt elimination is one thing. Doing it is another. That's why I built a Debt Elimination Worksheet for you. It's available for download, with instructions included at the back of this book.

Use it to:

- List every debt with balances, rates, and payments.
- Choose your strategy (snowball or avalanche).
- Track progress month by month.
- Redirect every freed dollar into savings and investments.

Don't just read this chapter. Go to the appendix, grab the worksheet, and put it into action. Every payment you kill is a step toward financial freedom.

9.
Investing That Actually Works

Investing isn't gambling, it's ownership. Stop chasing hype and learn how compounding wealth actually happens.

Most people think investing is gambling. They see headlines about stock market crashes, bubbles bursting, or crypto coins evaporating overnight, and they conclude that investing is risky, unpredictable, and dangerous. They imagine Wall Street traders yelling into phones, screens flashing red, fortunes made and lost in minutes.

That picture is wrong.

Investing isn't gambling. Gambling is putting money into a system designed for you to lose. Investing is ownership. When you invest, you're buying pieces of productive businesses, real estate, or systems that create value. You're not rolling dice. You're becoming an owner.

Owners get paid when businesses grow, when workers produce, when systems expand. Workers earn wages. Owners earn profits. This is why the wealthy always own. The formula is simple: if you only trade time for money, your earning power stops when you stop working. But if you own productive assets, they keep working for you, day and night, whether you show up or not.

The problem is that most people approach investing like a casino. They buy stocks because of hot tips from a friend. They chase hype like meme stocks, crypto fads, or day-trading systems sold online that promise quick riches. They speculate on lottery ticket options disguised as investments. That's not investing. That's gambling. Gambling keeps people poor.

Real investing is different. It's not about chasing fast money. It's not about guessing what will happen next week. It's about steady, disciplined, repetitive ownership. From the outside, it may look boring. But boring works. Boring compounds. Boring, done long enough, makes you free.

Compounding: The Engine of Wealth

Compounding is the quiet force that turns small amounts into life-changing wealth. Albert Einstein supposedly called it the eighth wonder of the world. Whether he said it or not, the point stands. Compounding is the reason ordinary people can build extraordinary wealth without lottery tickets, luck, or huge incomes.

The basic principle is: your money earns money. Then that money earns money. Over time, the snowball of wealth grows bigger and bigger. The earlier you start the snowball, the more unstoppable it becomes.

The Math of Compounding

Unless otherwise stated, all long-term return examples use a simplified 7 percent annual return to show realistic compounding.

Example 1: $100 per month
- 10 years = ~$17,000
- 20 years = ~$52,000
- 30 years = ~$122,000
- 40 years = ~$255,000

You contributed $48,000 over 40 years. Compounding added more than $200,000 on top. Your money did more work than you did.

Example 2: $500 per month
- 10 years = ~$85,000
- 20 years = ~$260,000
- 30 years = ~$610,000
- 40 years = ~$1.27 million

You contributed $240,000. Compounding turned it into over $1.2 million. That's how millionaires are built. Not from lottery wins, but from time and consistency.

Example 3: Early vs. Late Investor

- Maria invests $200 a month from ages 20 to 30. Total invested = $24,000. She stops, but leaves the money invested.

- James invests $200 a month from ages 30 to 60. Total invested = $72,000.

At age 60:
- Maria has ~$300,000.
- James has ~$245,000.

Maria invested one-third the money, but because she started earlier, her money worked longer. Compounding rewarded her more than James, even though he put in three times as much.

The lesson: **time and consistency matter more than timing.** Trying to guess the perfect day to invest is a distraction. The earlier you start and the longer you stay consistent, the more the compounding does the heavy lifting for you.

Why Compounding Works
Think of it like planting a tree. At first, it looks small and slow. After a year, you barely see growth. After five years, it starts to shade a corner of the yard. After 20 years, it is massive and produces fruit. Compounding is the same. At first, it feels like nothing is happening. Then suddenly, the growth becomes obvious – and unstoppable.

This is why people who delay saving or investing say, "I'll start later when I have more." Later never works. You can't make up lost time, no matter how much money you throw at it later. Compounding rewards the early, the patient, and the disciplined.

The Compounding Timeline
Most people underestimate what small, steady investing really does over decades. To make it clear, let's walk through what happens when you put money to work at an average 7 percent annual return.

Scenario 1: $100 per month
- **5 years** → ~$7,100

- **10 years** → ~$17,000
- **20 years** → ~$52,000
- **30 years** → ~$122,000
- **40 years** → ~$262,000

You only contributed $48,000 total. Compounding added more than $200,000.

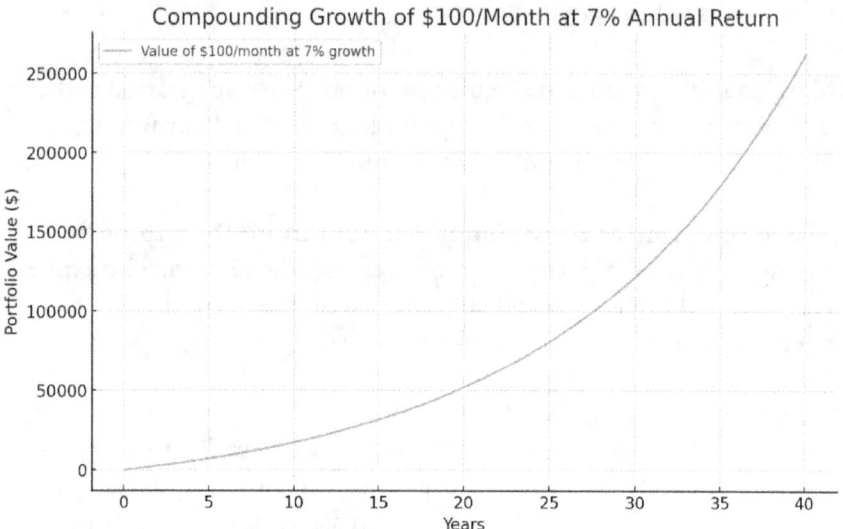

The Power of Compounding

Investing $100 each month at 7% annual growth turns $48,000 of contributions into over $260,000 over 20 years.

Scenario 2: $500 per month
- **5 years** → ~$36,000
- **10 years** → ~$86,000
- **20 years** → ~$260,000
- **30 years** → ~$610,000
- **40 years** → ~$1.31 million

You contributed $240,000. Compounding gave you over $1 million extra.

Scenario 3: $1,000 per month

- **5 years** → ~$71,000
- **10 years** → ~$173,000
- **20 years** → ~$521,000
- **30 years** → ~$1.22 million
- **40 years** → ~$2.62 million

You contributed $480,000. Compounding more than quadrupled it.

The Visual Pattern

- The first **5–10 years** feel slow. The numbers don't look exciting yet.

- By **20 years**, growth starts to show. The balance is multiple times your contributions.

- By **30 years**, the snowball is huge. Growth each year is bigger than your original contributions.

- By **40 years**, compounding is doing almost all the work. Your money is growing faster than you can earn.

The Lesson
The earlier you start, the more the timeline works in your favor. Waiting even 5 or 10 years means giving up hundreds of thousands (and even millions) that compounding could have created for you.

Wealth isn't built on big, dramatic wins. It's built on **small, boring, consistent actions repeated for decades.**

Gambling vs. Investing
Most people blur the line between gambling and investing because both involve money and uncertainty. But once you see the difference, it's crystal clear.

Gambling Looks Like This:

- Buying lottery tickets, hoping luck will change your life.

- Day trading without knowledge, jumping in and out of stocks like a roulette wheel.

- Chasing hype like meme stocks or unproven crypto coins that have no profits, no products, and no long-term value.

- Reacting to headlines with fear or greed – selling when markets crash, buying when they surge.

Gambling is emotional. It's about quick thrills and fast outcomes. The gambler asks: *What will this be worth tomorrow?*

Investing Looks Like This:

- Buying ownership in productive businesses that make products, provide services, and generate real profits.

- Holding assets for decades and letting time do the heavy lifting.

- Reinvesting dividends so your money earns money.

- Ignoring short-term noise and trusting the math of compounding.

Investing is rational. It's about discipline, patience, and ownership. The investor asks: *What will this be worth in 20 years?*

That one shift from tomorrow-thinking to decade-thinking separates those who build wealth from those who lose it.

Common Myths About Investing

1. **"I don't have enough to start."**
   Wrong. Today you can start with as little as $100, sometimes even less with fractional shares available in certain brokerage firms. Waiting until you "have enough" is how you lose the most valuable ingredient in wealth building: time.

2. **"The market is too risky."**
   Wrong. Over the last 100 years, despite recessions, depressions, wars, and crashes, the S&P 500 has averaged close to 10 percent annually. The real risk is not the market itself. It's you panicking, selling low, and locking in losses.

3. **"Investing is for the rich."**
   Wrong. Investing is how people become rich. Every wealthy family started somewhere. Waiting until you're already wealthy to invest is like waiting until you're in shape to start going to the gym.

4. **"I will wait until the market is safe."**
   Wrong. There is no "safe" time. The market always looks scary. The only thing that works is *time in the market*, not trying to time it.

Investment Vehicles Explained

People tune out sometimes when they hear financial jargon, so let's strip it down.

- **Stocks** → Ownership in a company. Buy Apple stock, and you literally own a piece of Apple. If it grows, so does your piece.

- **Bonds** → A loan. You lend money to a company or government, and they pay you interest. Less risky, but slower growth.

- **Mutual Funds** → Pooled money managed by professionals. Some are fine, but most charge high fees that eat your returns.

- **Index Funds** → Funds that simply match the market (like the S&P 500). They are cheap, simple, and effective.

- **ETFs (Exchange-Traded Funds)** → Similar to index funds but trade like stocks. They are flexible, low-cost, and often the best choice for everyday investors.

- **Dividends** → Cash payments companies make to shareholders. Reinvesting dividends is like putting compounding on steroids.

- **Retirement Accounts:**
  - **401(k):** Employer-sponsored. Pre-tax contributions lower your taxable income. Many employers match contributions. That match is *free money*.

  - **Traditional IRA:** Pre-tax contributions. Grows tax-deferred. Taxes are paid when you withdraw in retirement.

  - **Roth IRA:** After-tax contributions. Grows tax-free. Withdrawals in retirement are also tax-free. One of the best tools available.

  - **HSA (Health Savings Account):** Pre-tax contributions, tax-free growth, and tax-free withdrawals for medical expenses. A triple tax advantage.

Beginner Portfolios

In my first book, *How to Build Portfolios That Actually Work*, I explained why cookie-cutter models like the old 60/40 fail modern investors. Real portfolios need balance between **growth, income, and preservation.**

Even beginners can apply this balance with simple starter portfolios.

If you have $100 per month:
- $60 into a broad U.S. equity ETF (growth).
- $20 into a dividend ETF (income).
- $20 into a bond ETF (preservation).

If you have $1,000 per month:
- $500 into a U.S. equity ETF.
- $200 into a dividend ETF or REIT ETF for income.
- $200 into an international ETF for diversification.
- $100 into a bond ETF.

If you have $10,000 to invest at once:
- $5,000 into a U.S. equity ETF.
- $2,000 into a dividend ETF or REIT ETF.
- $2,000 into an international ETF.
- $1,000 into a bond ETF.

Optional: Set aside 5 to 10 percent for a tactical "satellite" - a sector or theme you believe in, like technology, infrastructure, or energy. But the bulk stays in your core allocation.

The lesson: balance matters. Growth without income is fragile. Income without preservation is risky. Preservation without growth is stagnation. Together, they work.

Mini Worksheet: Beginner Portfolio Preview
Here's a simple starter allocation for $100 a month:
- $60 → U.S. stock index fund
- $20 → Dividend ETF
- $20 → Bond ETF

Beginner Portfolio Allocation ($100/month) fund

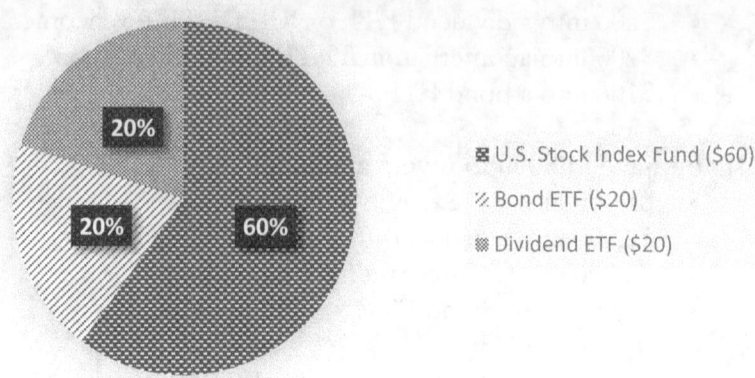

- ⊞ U.S. Stock Index Fund ($60)
- ⁒ Bond ETF ($20)
- ※ Dividend ETF ($20)

Beginner Portfolio Allocation:

A balanced $100 monthly investment split between U.S. stocks, dividend ETFs, and bonds provides growth, income, and stability.

➤ Full allocation charts and compounding growth charts are available for download in your Wealth Toolkit.

The Half Rule Applied to Investing

In Chapter 7 you learned the Half Rule: Save half, live on half. That rule isn't just about budgeting, it's about acceleration. When you apply it to investing, the timeline to financial independence shrinks dramatically.

Example: A household earns $80,000 a year. Instead of living on $70,000 like most people, they commit to living on $40,000 and saving the other $40,000. That single choice changes everything. They invest in the balanced portfolio outlined earlier: U.S. equity ETF, dividend ETF, international ETF, and bonds. At a 7 percent growth rate, in just 15 years they can reach financial independence.

Most Americans never reach that point even after 40 years of work.

The Half Rule forces cash flow discipline. The portfolio provides growth, income, and preservation. Together they create a system that guarantees progress. One controls today. The other builds tomorrow.

The Psychology of Investors

Successful investing has less to do with math and more to do with behavior. The math works if you give it time. The challenge is whether you can stay disciplined while the world tempts you to do the wrong thing.

Wealthy investors think differently:

- They don't panic when markets fall. They see crashes as temporary sales opportunities, not permanent losses.

- They don't chase hype. They know steady companies with consistent profits will outlast the fads.

- They don't sell out of fear. They stay invested and let compounding do the work.

- They don't obsess over today's price. They think in decades, not days.

Poor investors do the opposite. They panic when markets dip, sell low, and then buy high when the headlines pump a "can't-miss" stock. They gamble instead of own.

Emotional investors lose. Patient investors win.

Case Studies

These examples illustrate that wealth doesn't come from income alone. It comes from behavior. Four people can earn similar amounts and end up with completely different results based on the decisions they make month after month. Their stories illustrate what works, and what doesn't.

Case 1: The Saver
Maya starts small. At 22, she invests $100 a month into the balanced beginner portfolio. By age 62 she has over $250,000. She only contributed $48,000 herself. Compounding added almost $200,000.

Case 2: The Builder
James invests $1,000 a month starting at 30. By 60, he has over $1.2 million. Half came from his contributions, half from compounding.

Case 3: The Gambler
Daniel chases hype stocks and crypto. He wins a few big wins but loses more. After 10 years, his $60,000 of contributions are only worth $30,000.

Case 4: The Owner
Lisa invests $500 a month in the balanced portfolio. After 10 years, she has almost $90,000. After 30 years, over $600,000. She never had to outsmart the market. She just owned it.

The Investing Roadmap
Investing feels intimidating until you break it into stages. Like debt elimination, it works best step by step.

Stage 1 (0–12 months): Getting started
- Open your first account, either a brokerage or retirement account.

- Begin with $100–$200 a month in the balanced beginner portfolio.

- Focus less on perfect choices and more on building the habit.

Stage 2 (1–5 years): Building momentum
- Increase contributions as income rises.

- Add international and income-focused funds for balance.

- Max out retirement accounts like a 401(k) or Roth IRA for tax advantages.

Stage 3 (5–15 years): Accelerating growth
- Automate half of income into investments.

- Stay diversified between growth, income, and preservation.

- Reinvest dividends instead of cashing them out.

Stage 4 (15+ years): Reaping rewards
- Compounding accelerates rapidly. Growth takes on a life of its own.

- Dividends and interest begin covering lifestyle expenses.

- Financial independence becomes reality. Work becomes optional.

Action Plan: Your First $100
You don't need thousands to begin. You only need action.

Take $100 and invest it this month.
- $60 in a U.S. equity ETF for growth.
- $20 in a dividend ETF for income.
- $20 in a bond ETF for preservation.

Automate the contribution every month and do not ever stop.

That $100 habit grows into thousands. Thousands grow into hundreds of thousands. Ownership builds wealth. Gambling keeps you poor.

Start now. Plant the seed. Let compounding grow the forest.

10.
Build Multiple Streams of Income

One paycheck is never enough. Wealth is built on creating income streams that protect you, grow you, and free you.

Relying on one paycheck is like building a house on a single pillar. It might hold for a while, but the first real storm can bring it down. That's the financial life most people live: all their bills, savings, and plans rest on one fragile source of income.

The problem isn't hard to see. If that paycheck disappears, everything disappears. A layoff. A medical emergency. A company restructuring. A business closure. Any of these can take away your entire safety net in an instant.

Wealthy people see the risk differently. They understand that real security comes from diversification, not just in investments, but in income itself. They layer income streams. They add one after another until their financial house has many pillars, not one. If an income stream dries up, the others keep flowing. That's why they stay free while others stay vulnerable.

Why One Paycheck Is Fragile

Think about your life right now. Rent or mortgage, car payment, food, utilities, gas, insurance, phone, subscriptions, childcare... Those demands show up every month without fail. Now imagine your single paycheck disappears. How long before the bills bury you?

For most Americans, the answer is measured in weeks, not months. Surveys show nearly 60 percent can't cover a $1,000 emergency without debt.[37] That's what paycheck dependence looks like. It doesn't matter if the paycheck is $40,000 a year or $400,000. If it's your only income stream, you're fragile.

One paycheck means your financial life is controlled by someone else. A boss deciding if you stay employed. A client deciding if they keep paying you. An economy deciding if your industry survives. That isn't freedom. That's dependency.

The wealthy never rely on one source. They build layers. They make sure if one stream falls, others catch them. That's what makes them durable.

Active Income vs Passive Income
To build multiple streams, you need to know the difference between active and passive.

Active Income
Active income requires you to show up. If you stop working, the money stops. Salaries, hourly wages, freelance projects, consulting, and most small businesses fall into this category. Active income is important because it gets you started, but it's fragile by itself.

Passive Income
Passive income comes from ownership. You buy, build, or set up something once, and it continues to produce income with little daily involvement. Dividends, rental income, royalties, affiliate businesses, and automated systems all qualify. Passive income isn't magic. It takes time, capital, and risk to build. But once established, it keeps flowing even when you stop working.

Wealthy people use active income to buy passive income. They start by working for money, but they finish by letting money work for them.

The Five Major Streams of Income
There are hundreds of creative ways to make money, but almost every method fits into one of five categories. Wealthy people understand these categories and intentionally build streams in each one.

1. Income from Work
This is where almost everyone begins. You trade time for money. It covers salaries, hourly work, overtime, tips, commissions, and

freelance work. Work income is essential because it gives you the seed money to create everything else. The goal isn't to stay here forever. The goal is to convert earned income into ownership income as quickly as possible. Work income is the fuel that builds assets.

2. Income from Business

Business income comes from something you own. It might be a one-person consulting operation or a full company with staff and systems. Some businesses depend heavily on the owner. Others can eventually run without daily involvement. That's where true leverage begins. A business creates scalability, control, and the ability to earn far beyond what a single paycheck can provide.

3. Income from Investments

Investment income is the quiet engine of long-term wealth. Stocks, index funds, bonds, REITs, ETFs, and other assets work while you sleep. Growth compounds year after year. Dividends and interest build passive income. This is the stream wealthy people treat with the most respect because it becomes the foundation of their freedom.

4. Income from Real Estate

Real estate offers two powerful forms of wealth building. First, cash flow from rent. Second, appreciation over time. Rental properties, small multifamily units, commercial buildings, short-term rentals, and house hacks all fall into this category. Real estate often outpaces inflation, which means it preserves and grows wealth even when the market changes.

5. Income from Side Hustles

Side hustles are entry-level businesses. They begin active but often evolve into semi-passive income streams. Examples include online stores, tutoring, digital products, affiliate marketing, photography, and service-based work. Many successful entrepreneurs began with a side hustle that eventually turned into a significant income stream.

Wealthy people rarely rely on just one or two streams. They intentionally stack these streams because each one multiplies the others.

The Psychology of Single-Stream Thinking

Most people stop at one paycheck because it feels predictable. A paycheck arrives every two weeks, and predictability feels like safety. The truth is that a single income source is fragile. One layoff, one health issue, one market shift, and everything falls apart.

People cling to single-stream thinking because the alternatives require discomfort. Learning a new skill, building a business, investing consistently, or managing a rental property all feel intimidating at first. Many prefer familiar stress over temporary discomfort.

Wealthy people do the opposite. They accept short-term discomfort to build long-term security. They give up a little convenience to create future freedom. They build streams that outlast job changes, company failures, and economic uncertainty.

Comfort creates stagnation. Multiple income streams create freedom.

Deep Dive: Breaking Down the Five Streams

Here's a closer look at each stream, how it works, and how wealthy people use it.

Work Income: Making Your Paycheck Work for You

Work income is where you learn discipline. Wealthy people know that earned income isn't the end goal. It's the launchpad. They treat every paycheck as an opportunity to fund the next stage of wealth building.

With work income, the focus isn't how much you earn. The focus is how much you keep and where it goes. A portion goes toward living. A portion goes toward investing. A portion goes toward building or buying assets. The paycheck is the tool, not the destination.

Examples:
- A teacher investing ten percent of every paycheck
- A nurse contributing to a 401(k) and Roth IRA
- A contractor funneling profits into a rental property down payment

Work income creates opportunity. What you do with that opportunity determines your future.

Business Income: Scaling Beyond Your Time
Business income is the most misunderstood stream. Many people think a business simply replaces a job. Wealthy people see it differently. A business is a system designed to multiply effort. Good businesses create value even when the owner is not present.

Business income breaks the link between hours worked and dollars earned. That's why this stream can grow faster than any other.

Examples:
- A consultant who later hires subcontractors
- A small online product that scales without extra labor
- A local service business that expands through employees
- A digital course that sells repeatedly after it is created

Business income creates leverage. It turns time into a multiplier instead of a limit.

Investment Income: Ownership Over Speculation
Investment income rewards patience and discipline. This stream grows quietly at first, then aggressively over time. Wealthy people understand that consistent investing beats timing the market. Ownership is the goal. Compounding is the method.

Investment income doesn't require prediction. It requires consistency.

Examples:
- Index fund portfolios that compound year after year
- Dividend stocks that pay cash distributions
- Bonds that produce steady interest
- Automated investment contributions every paycheck

Investments are the backbone of financial independence. They grow while you sleep, while you work, and while you live your life.

Real Estate Income: Cash Flow Plus Appreciation
Real estate is one of the oldest and most reliable wealth-building tools. It provides income today and value growth tomorrow. It also allows you to control a large asset with a smaller initial investment through financing.

Wealthy people use real estate to create steady, inflation-protected income.

Examples:
- House hacking a duplex where tenants cover most of the mortgage
- Buying a rental that earns cash flow each month
- Purchasing a commercial property with strong long-term value
- Investing in small multifamily units for diversified rents

Real estate is powerful because tenants effectively pay the mortgage for you. Over time, you gain ownership, cash flow, and appreciation.

Side Hustle Income: The Starter Stream
Side hustles are how many people start building additional streams without quitting their job. The purpose of a side hustle is not to stay small. The purpose is to gain skills, test ideas, create income, and eventually convert it into a scalable stream.

Many major businesses began as simple side hustles. The learning, consistency, and confidence gained from a small side stream often lead to larger opportunities.

Examples:
- Selling products online
- Offering tutoring or coaching
- Creating content that earns ad revenue

- Developing digital products or templates
- Freelance writing, design, or consulting

Side hustles prove that you can create income on your own terms.

How the Wealthy Stack Streams
The wealthy layer income like an architect builds floors on a skyscraper. They don't stop with one.

- A doctor may earn a salary, but also own rental properties and a portfolio of dividend stocks.

- An entrepreneur may pay themselves a wage, while also collecting profits from the company and dividends from investments.

- An author may earn royalties from books, speaking fees, and income from courses.

Each stream makes them less dependent on the others.

The Half Rule Applied
From Chapter 7 you know the Half Rule: save half, live on half. This rule accelerates the creation of new streams.

- Save half → invest in stocks. Dividends create the second stream.

- Save half → buy rental property. Rent creates the third stream.

- Save half → start a side business. Profits create the fourth stream.

Every dollar saved is a seed. Over time you don't just grow one tree. You grow an orchard.

Building Your Own Income Map

Multiple streams of income are designed, not accidental. You can design yours step by step.

Step 1: Identify Current Streams
List your paycheck, freelance, or any side hustles. See what you already have.

Step 2: Identify Gaps
What happens if your main source disappears? What's missing?

Step 3: Build Incrementally
Add one stream at a time. Start small. Don't chase five at once.

Step 4: Automate Growth
Automate savings, investments, and business systems so they grow without constant effort.

Step 5: Review Annually
Every year, map your income streams. Are they stronger? Are they balanced?

The Income Map Roadmap

Stage 1 (0–12 months)
- Build emergency fund.
- Start investing $100–$200 monthly.
- Experiment with a side hustle.

Stage 2 (1–5 years)
- Grow side hustle into steady stream.
- Expand investments.
- Save for a real estate down payment.

Stage 3 (5–10 years)
- Add rental property.
- Automate half of income into investments.
- Build small business systems.

Stage 4 (10+ years)
- Portfolio produces dividends.
- Real estate produces cash flow.
- Side businesses or royalties generate passive income.
- Work income becomes optional.

Action Plan: Design Your Income Map
One paycheck is fragile. Multiple streams create freedom.

Your challenge today: design your income map. Write down your current streams. Add at least one new stream to build within the next 12 months. Maybe it's a side hustle. Maybe it's an investment account. Maybe it's a rental property.

Don't wait for someone else to secure your future. Build streams. Build ownership. Build freedom.

11.
Taxes, Protection, and Smart Structures

Learn how to structure taxes and insurance intentionally to protect what you build and keep more of what you earn.

Building wealth is hard. Keeping it is harder.

Most people think that once they have savings in the bank, investments in the market, or a nice house in the suburbs, they're safe. They're not. Wealth is fragile when it isn't protected. One lawsuit, one accident, one illness, or one unplanned tax bill can wipe out what took years to build.

Wealthy people understand this better than anyone. That's why they spend as much time on defense as they do on offense. They don't just focus on making money. They focus on keeping it. They use insurance, legal structures, estate plans, and tax strategies to make sure their money stays theirs.

If you don't protect what you build, you're leaving the door open for someone else to take it.

Why Protection Matters

You can spend decades saving, investing, and working hard. But wealth can disappear in an instant if it isn't defended.

- A car accident leaves you liable for damages. Without proper liability coverage, your savings and even your house are exposed.

- An illness racks up six-figure medical bills. Without health insurance, everything you own goes to hospitals.

- A lawsuit targets your business or personal assets. Without legal separation, your accounts and property are wide open.

- Inflation eats away at your cash. Without growth-oriented investments, your "safe" money loses value every year.

- Taxes drain your gains. Without strategy, you overpay and lose thousands unnecessarily.

Protection isn't optional. It's part of wealth. Wealth without protection isn't really wealth.

The Enemies of Wealth
There are three main enemies of wealth: risk, taxes, and time. They are constant. They never take a break. If you ignore them, they eat what you build. If you prepare for them, you can keep growing.

Risk
Risk is everything that can go wrong in life. It's the unpredictable, the "what if," the events you don't see coming. Illness, accidents, lawsuits, disability, natural disasters, divorce, or even business failure.

One lawsuit can wipe out your savings. One medical emergency can drain a decade of progress. A storm can destroy property you worked years to buy. You can't live without risk, but you can prepare for it. Insurance, legal structures, and cash reserves are the shields that keep risk from becoming ruin.

Think of it this way: wealth isn't just about what you gain. It's about what you keep. If you ignore risk, you're gambling with your future.

Taxes
Taxes are the government's cut. Earn a paycheck, you get taxed. Sell an asset, you get taxed. Buy property, you pay property taxes every year. Die, and your heirs get taxed again through estate taxes.

Without planning, taxes can quietly take 30 to 50 percent of your lifetime earnings. That means if you earn $2 million across your career, $600,000 to $1 million could disappear to the IRS and state governments. With planning, you can reduce, defer, or even eliminate much of that burden.

This is why the wealthy focus so much on tax strategy. They use retirement accounts, Roth conversions, trusts, real estate deductions, business structures, and charitable giving to keep more of what they earn. They don't cheat. They plan. The poor hand over their money without question.

Taxes aren't just a bill. They're an enemy that grows stronger every year if you ignore it.

Time

Time is the most underestimated enemy of wealth. Time wears everything down. Inflation erodes your purchasing power year after year. Neglect erodes your financial plan when you forget to update it. Complacency erodes progress when you stop paying attention.

$100 today will not buy $100 worth of goods in 20 years. Inflation guarantees it. That "safe" savings account becomes weaker every year you leave money sitting idle. The longer you wait to invest or protect what you own, the harder it becomes to catch up.

Time is sneaky. Risk and taxes announce themselves loudly. Time destroys silently in the background. It takes no effort from you. If you don't maintain defenses against it, time will destroy what you built.

Wealth doesn't just die from bad decisions. It also dies from neglect.

Insurance: The Armor

Insurance isn't exciting. Nobody brags about their policies at dinner. But insurance is armor. It shields you from risks that could otherwise wipe out years of progress in a single blow. The poor see insurance as an expense they "can't afford." The wealthy see it as protection they can't live without.

The difference is perspective.

Without insurance, one bad event can undo everything you've built. With it, you take risks on your terms. You can focus on growth knowing that your foundation is secure.

Health Insurance
Medical bills are the number one cause of bankruptcy in America. A single surgery or extended hospital stay can cost more than your house. Even if you live a healthy lifestyle, accidents and illnesses happen without warning. Health insurance is not optional.

If premiums for comprehensive plans feel high, consider a high-deductible health plan paired with a Health Savings Account (HSA). The HSA lets you save pre-tax dollars for medical expenses and grow those funds tax-free. That way, you protect yourself against unlimited medical costs while building a reserve for the future.

The uninsured gamble with their future every day. Wealthy people never take that gamble.

Disability Insurance
Your ability to earn income is your biggest asset. If you make $80,000 a year, that's $4 million over 50 years of work – before raises, bonuses, or investments. If you lose that ability, you lose everything. Disability insurance is income insurance.

Short-term coverage helps for a few months. Long-term coverage is the real key, because many disabling conditions last for years. A car accident, a chronic illness, or even stress-related conditions can end a career overnight.

Most employers offer basic disability insurance, but it's rarely enough. Wealthy households often add their own private coverage to ensure that if income stops, their wealth plan doesn't collapse.

Life Insurance
If someone depends on your income, you need life insurance. A spouse, children, or aging parents rely on you more than you realize. Without life insurance, your death can leave them with bills, debt, and no financial safety net. That financial pressure can destroy everything you worked for.

For most households, **term life insurance** is the right choice. It's simple, affordable, and provides a large amount of coverage for a very low cost. A healthy thirty-five-year-old can often buy one million dollars of coverage for less than fifty dollars a month. You get the protection your family needs without draining your budget.

Permanent life insurance has specific uses, but it's not a requirement for most people. It can be helpful in advanced estate planning or for very high net worth households with tax or inheritance needs. But for the average family, the extra cost is unnecessary and often harmful. Most people simply don't need permanent policies.

The real purpose of life insurance is protection during the years when your family can't afford to lose you financially. If you plan correctly, you won't need the insurance forever. When you invest consistently and build liquid assets, those investments can eventually replace the need for a policy. By the time a thirty-year term expires, a disciplined saver and investor should have enough net worth to self-insure. In other words, your portfolio can act as the safety net once your policy ends.

Life insurance isn't for you. It's for the people who rely on your income and depend on you to protect their future. Your job is to make sure they're safe even if you aren't here to provide for them.

Auto Insurance

Auto accidents are common and costly. If you cause one, you could be sued for damages far beyond the cost of your car. Liability coverage is the real key. Don't skimp on it. Carrying only the state minimum is financial suicide.

One serious accident can lead to a lawsuit that drains savings, retirement accounts, or even your home. Auto insurance protects your assets from being taken in a single event. Comprehensive and collision coverage matter too, but liability is what guards your wealth.

Homeowners or Renters Insurance

Your home is one of your largest assets, and one of your biggest risks. Fires, theft, natural disasters, or even a visitor slipping on your porch can leave you exposed. Homeowners or renters insurance protects you from both property damage and liability.

Too many people focus only on replacing their belongings. The real value of these policies is liability coverage. If someone sues you for an injury on your property, this coverage pays before your personal assets are touched.

Umbrella Insurance

Umbrella insurance is one of the most underrated protections available. For just a few hundred dollars a year, you can add $1 million or more in liability coverage above your auto and home policies.

If you're sued for damages that exceed your standard coverage, the umbrella policy steps in. It protects your assets, your income, and your future. Wealthy families almost always carry umbrella coverage because lawsuits are more common the more successful you become.

It's one of the best deals in insurance and one of the easiest ways to create true peace of mind.

Mini Worksheet: Protection Quick Check

Do you already have these covered?

- Health insurance
- Term life insurance (if you have dependents)
- Auto insurance with liability coverage
- Renters or homeowners insurance
- A will in place

➤ A full Protection Checklist is available for download in your Wealth Toolkit.

The Cash Defense: Emergency Fund Reminder

Insurance protects you from big risks. But what about the smaller ones? A broken transmission, a slow sales quarter, or an unexpected medical bill can wreck your finances if you don't have cash reserves ready.

That's why the emergency fund matters. It's your first line of defense before insurance ever comes into play.

- If you earn a salary: keep at least three months of living expenses in cash.

- If you earn commissions or run a business: keep six to twelve months of living expenses in cash.

This reserve fund isn't for investing. It's not for vacations. It's not for "I want a new TV." It's only for emergencies. Keep it liquid in a high-yield savings account or money market account.

Without it, the first bump in the road forces you into debt and destroys the progress you worked so hard to build.

Legal Structures: Shields Around Your Assets
Wealthy people don't keep all assets in their personal name. They know that one lawsuit, one creditor, or one bad business deal can threaten everything they've worked for. Instead, they use legal structures to create barriers between risk and wealth. Think of these structures like walls around a castle. Even if one wall is breached, the whole castle doesn't fall.

LLCs (Limited Liability Companies)
An LLC is one of the most common tools for protecting assets. When you form an LLC for your business, the company becomes its own legal entity. That means if the business is sued (for example, a customer slips on your property or a client claims damages) your personal bank account, house, and investments are shielded.

Without an LLC, the lawsuit comes after *you*. With an LLC, it stops at the business. This separation is why many real estate investors often

151

hold each rental property in its own LLC. If a tenant sues over one property, the others remain protected.

LLCs are also flexible for taxes. By default, profits flow through to your personal return, but with the right setup you may elect S-Corp status for additional tax advantages.

Trusts

Trusts aren't just for the ultra-wealthy. They're tools anyone can use to control how assets are handled during life and after death. Trusts also let you control timing. Instead of leaving your children a lump sum at age 18, you can stagger inheritance over decades, ensuring money is used wisely long after you're gone.

Corporations

Corporations take separation even further. Unlike an LLC, which is usually tied closely to one person or a small group, corporations create a distinct entity that exists beyond the owners. If the company is sued, the corporation is responsible, not the individual shareholders.

Corporations also offer unique tax planning opportunities. They can retain earnings, pay dividends, and in some cases offer deductions that individuals can't. Business owners who plan carefully can use corporate structures to protect personal wealth, reinvest profits, and limit personal liability.

For high-risk industries (construction, healthcare, finance) corporations are often essential. They allow the business to take on risk while the owners' personal assets stay safe.

Why Structures Matter

One lawsuit can take everything if you're unprotected. Imagine a small business owner who runs everything in their own name. A single customer lawsuit could bankrupt them personally and wipe out retirement savings. Now imagine the same business inside an LLC, with the owner's home and investments shielded. The problem stays contained.

Wealthy people never assume "it won't happen to me." They build structures so that *when* something happens, the damage is limited.

Your personal nest egg shouldn't be exposed to the risks of your business. Your real estate portfolio shouldn't all be lumped under your personal name. The more you build, the more you need shields.

Estate Planning: Protecting Your Family

Estate planning isn't just for the wealthy. It's for anyone who wants control over what happens to their money, their healthcare, and their family when they are gone or incapacitated. Without an estate plan, the government decides for you, and those decisions are rarely in your family's best interest. Estate planning isn't about death. It's about peace of mind. It ensures that your loved ones are protected and that the wealth you worked so hard to build does not disappear in legal fees, taxes, or family disputes.

Wills

A will is the most basic estate planning tool. It states who gets what when you pass. Without one, the state steps in, appoints someone to handle your estate, and decides who inherits. That process is called probate, and it can take years, cost thousands in legal fees, and will expose your private finances to the public record.

Even worse, dying without a will (called "intestate") means your assets may go to people you never intended. For example, an estranged relative could end up inheriting everything while a close friend or stepchild gets nothing. A simple will prevents that outcome.

Trusts

Trusts go a step further. They avoid probate, provide privacy, and give you control long after you are gone. A trust is essentially a set of instructions written in legal form. You appoint a trustee to carry them out.

- **Revocable Trusts**: Also called living trusts. These keep control in your hands while you are alive but allow assets to pass directly to heirs when you die. The main benefit is avoiding probate – the long, expensive public court process. With a revocable trust, your assets transfer smoothly and privately.

- **Irrevocable Trusts**: These remove assets from your personal ownership entirely. Because you no longer "own" them, they are shielded from lawsuits and estate taxes. For example, if someone sues you, assets in an irrevocable trust are typically untouchable. Wealthy families use these to protect generational wealth and reduce estate tax burdens.

Trusts also allow you to control *timing*. For example, instead of giving your child a lump sum at 18, the trust might release money at 25, 30, and 35, or tie distributions to milestones like graduating college. This prevents heirs from blowing through an inheritance and keeps wealth working across generations.

Beneficiary Designations

One of the most overlooked parts of estate planning are beneficiary forms. Retirement accounts, life insurance, and even some bank accounts pass directly by beneficiary designation, not by your will. That means if you wrote your will last year but forgot to update your 401(k) beneficiary from ten years ago, the old name wins.

Every year, families lose millions to ex-spouses, estranged relatives, or outdated beneficiaries. Review and update these forms every time there is a major life change: marriage, divorce, new child, or death in the family.

Power of Attorney

A power of attorney gives someone the authority to act for you if you can't. Imagine you're in a coma after an accident. Without a power of attorney, your spouse or children may need to go to court just to pay your bills or access accounts. With a power of attorney, they can step in immediately.

Choose someone you trust completely. This person may control finances, sign legal documents, or make other binding decisions on your behalf.

Healthcare Directive

Also called a living will, this document spells out your medical wishes if you are incapacitated. Do you want life support? For how long? What about organ donation? These are difficult conversations, but leaving them unanswered forces your family to guess, and usually argue. A healthcare directive removes the burden and ensures your wishes are followed.

Why It Matters

Estate planning prevents chaos. Without it, your family faces court delays, higher taxes, and painful uncertainty. With it, they have clarity, protection, and stability.

Think of estate planning as the final piece of wealth building. You spend years working, saving, and investing. Estate planning makes sure it doesn't all disappear the moment you're gone.

Taxes: The Silent Killer

Taxes are one of the biggest drags on wealth. You work, you earn, you save, you invest. The government takes a cut at every stage. Earn a paycheck, you pay income tax. Sell an investment, you pay capital gains tax. Pass wealth to your heirs, they pay estate tax. Even owning property means an annual bill that never goes away.

Most people accept taxes passively. They complain, but they do nothing to reduce the burden. Wealthy people take the opposite approach. They plan. They use the tax code to their advantage. They understand that every dollar saved in taxes is a dollar that compounds for them instead of disappearing.

Income Taxes

For most people, income taxes are the largest recurring expense. Yet too many people leave free money on the table. Tax-advantaged accounts are the first line of defense.

- **401(k)**: Contribute pre-tax, lower your taxable income today, and grow investments tax-deferred. Many employers also match contributions, and that match is literally free money.

- **Roth IRA**: Pay tax upfront, then grow and withdraw tax-free. This is especially powerful for younger investors who expect higher taxes in the future.

- **HSA (Health Savings Account)**: Triple benefit. Contributions are tax-deductible, growth is tax-free, and withdrawals for medical expenses are also tax-free.

Every dollar you can move into these accounts not only lowers today's tax bill but also shields your money for decades of compounding. It's also important to note that tax laws change and not every strategy applies to every income level. Always confirm eligibility with a tax professional.

Capital Gains Taxes
Too many investors sabotage themselves by selling too soon. Sell before one year, and your profit is taxed at higher short-term rates, often the same as ordinary income. Hold longer than a year, and you qualify for long-term capital gains rates, which are far lower.

Wealthy investors understand patience. They buy quality, hold it, and let time do the work. They also use **tax-loss harvesting**: strategically selling losing investments to offset gains. This reduces taxable income and keeps more money compounding.

Don't treat your portfolio like a revolving door. Every trade has tax consequences.

Estate Taxes
If your estate is large enough, the government will want another cut when you die. Without planning, your heirs may lose a significant portion of what you worked for. Wealthy families protect against this with tools like trusts, family gifting strategies, and charitable planning.

- **Trusts**: Move assets into revocable or irrevocable trusts to reduce exposure and control distribution.

- **Annual Gifting**: Give up to the annual gift tax exclusion to heirs while you're alive, lowering your taxable estate.

- **Charitable Giving**: Donating to charities or foundations reduces estate size and supports causes you care about.

Estate planning isn't just about where assets go. It's about how much of them actually make it there.

Property Taxes

Real estate comes with a bill that never disappears. Property taxes rise over time, and if you don't plan for them, they can choke cash flow. A rental property that looks profitable on paper can lose its shine once property taxes increase.

Wealthy investors plan property taxes into every deal. They know the local tax rates, anticipate increases, and set aside reserves so they're never caught off guard. Homeowners should do the same.

Why Taxes Matter

Taxes aren't random. They're predictable. You know income will be taxed. You know capital gains will be taxed. You know your estate will be taxed. You know property will be taxed.

The poor ignore this and hope it "works out." The wealthy plan ahead and keep more of what they earn. That difference compounds over decades into millions of dollars.

Inflation: The Constant Threat

Inflation isn't just an economic concept you hear on the news. It's a constant threat sitting in the background of your financial life. Every year, quietly and steadily, it eats away at the value of your money. A dollar today will not buy the same amount of groceries, gas, or housing ten years from now. That's the reality your money is fighting against.

Most people underestimate this. They think "prices just go up sometimes." But the truth is that inflation never stops. Even at a modest two to three percent per year, your money will lose almost half its buying power in 25 years. That means the $50,000 you keep sitting in a savings account today may only buy $25,000 worth of goods when you actually need it.

This is why cash is not a "safe investment". Cash feels safe because it does not swing up and down like the stock market. But "safe" cash is actually guaranteed loss. Every year you leave large amounts sitting idle, inflation is slowly destroying it.

You can't hide from inflation. You can't save your way out of it in a checking account or under a mattress. The only defense is offense. You need to own assets that grow faster than inflation.

- **Stocks**: Companies raise prices over time, and ownership in those companies means your wealth rises with them.

- **Real Estate**: Property values and rents increase alongside inflation, giving you both income and appreciation.

- **Businesses**: Whether your own business or investments in others, productive enterprises adapt to rising costs and pass them on to customers.

Growth is the shield. Growth is the only protection. Cash alone guarantees loss. Assets that grow guarantee survival.

Inflation is constant, so your defense against it must also be constant. Every month, every year, keep your money working. Don't confuse stillness with safety.

How the Wealthy Protect

Wealthy people understand something that most overlook: making money is only half the game. The other half is keeping it. Offense builds wealth, but defense preserves it. Without defense, one unexpected event can undo decades of progress. That's why wealthy families and business owners treat protection as part of their strategy, not as an afterthought.

They Insure Risks

The wealthy know they can't predict every accident, illness, or lawsuit, but they can prepare for them. They don't view insurance as a burden. They see it as armor. Health insurance prevents medical bills from wiping out savings. Disability insurance safeguards income if they can't work. Umbrella policies cover liability risks that could otherwise lead to million-dollar lawsuits. Where others see "just another premium," the wealthy see protection that keeps their empire standing.

They Separate Assets with LLCs and Trusts

Wealthy people rarely keep all assets in their personal name. They know that lawsuits, creditors, or even family disputes can attack exposed wealth. That's why they create legal shields. Businesses are owned inside LLCs or corporations. Properties are held in trusts. These structures act like walls around wealth, ensuring that a single accident or business problem can't bring everything down.

They Plan Estates to Protect Heirs

Estate planning isn't just paperwork. It's a shield for the next generation. Wealthy families put wills, trusts, and beneficiary designations in place so assets transfer smoothly. They avoid probate, minimize estate taxes, and prevent their children from inheriting chaos. They also control timing. Instead of dumping money into the hands of a 19-year-old, they may structure trusts that release funds in stages. This keeps the family wealth intact instead of gone in a few reckless years.

They Use Tax Strategies to Keep More

The wealthy know taxes are predictable. They'll be there every year, waiting to take a portion. Instead of ignoring them, they plan around them. They max out tax-advantaged accounts like 401(k)s, Roth IRAs, and HSAs. Business owners deduct legitimate expenses and use structures to reduce taxable income. Investors harvest tax losses strategically to offset gains. They don't evade taxes. They out-plan them. That planning is often the difference between keeping 70 percent of their gains or losing 40 percent of them.

They Invest to Stay Ahead of Inflation

Wealthy people never confuse cash with security. They keep cash for emergencies, but they don't sit on piles of idle money. They know inflation will eat it alive. Instead, they place their money in growth assets (stocks, real estate, businesses) that rise faster than prices. By staying invested, they ensure their purchasing power grows, not shrinks.

The Wealthy Don't Leave Wealth Unguarded

That's the core difference. The average person saves and spends with no shield in place. The wealthy never assume "it will all work out." They assume something will go wrong, and they prepare for it in advance. Their offense builds wealth, but their defense ensures it stays in the family for generations.

The Protection Roadmap

Stage 1 (0–12 months):
- Get health, auto, and renters or home insurance.
- Write a will.
- Build an emergency fund.

Stage 2 (1–5 years):
- Add term life insurance if you have dependents.
- Add disability insurance.
- Open an umbrella liability policy.
- Create an LLC for any business.

Stage 3 (5–10 years):
- Set up a revocable trust.
- Update beneficiary forms.
- Review tax strategy with a professional.

Stage 4 (10+ years):
- Add advanced estate planning (irrevocable trusts, gifting).

- Review protection annually.
- Train heirs in financial literacy.

Action Plan: Protect What You Build

Building wealth is only half the battle. Protecting it is the other half. Too many people spend their lives working, saving, and investing, only to lose it all because they left the back door wide open.

One lawsuit, one car accident, one medical bill, or one overlooked form can erase years of discipline.

Your challenge: create a **Protection Checklist** today. Not tomorrow. Not when you "get around to it." Today.

Ask yourself:
- Do I have health insurance that protects me from medical bankruptcy?

- Do I have auto insurance with liability and, if needed, an umbrella policy for extra protection?

- Do I have a will, a trust, and updated beneficiaries so my family doesn't face chaos when I'm gone?

- Is my business and real estate assets separated from your personal wealth through LLCs or corporations?

- Do I have a tax strategy in place so I keep more of what I earn instead of handing it all to the government?

If you answered "no" to any of these, then your wealth is exposed. It doesn't matter how hard you work or how much you save. Until you put defenses in place, your money is at risk of being taken.

Protecting your wealth isn't glamorous. It won't impress anyone at a dinner party. But it's what allows your wealth to last. This is the difference between families who build for generations and families who build once and lose it.

You worked hard to build. Don't let one accident, one lawsuit, or one tax bill take it away.

Part III –
Mastery and
Freedom

You've faced the truth about money myths. You've fought lifestyle creep. You've killed toxic debt. You've shifted your mindset, taken control of cash flow, and started investing the right way. You've built multiple streams of income and learned how to protect what you create.

Now comes the final stage: mastery.

Mastery is where offense and defense stop being separate games. It's where your systems run together like gears in a machine. Income grows automatically. Investments compound in the background. Risks are shielded. Your family is secure. You're no longer reacting to money. You're directing it.

Most people never get here. They stay trapped in survival, running paycheck to paycheck. Some make it to comfort, but comfort is fragile. Very few ever reach mastery.

Mastery isn't about having millions in the bank. It's about freedom. Freedom to choose how you spend your time. Freedom to walk away from a job you hate. Freedom to live without fear of bills, layoffs, or emergencies.

To reach mastery, you need to:

- Keep your systems simple and repeatable.

- Stay disciplined when everyone else panics.

- Continue investing through every season.

- Teach your family what you know so your wealth outlives you.

This section is about thinking and acting like someone who never slips back into being poor. These chapters are about staying wealthy, expanding beyond your job, and designing a life where money serves you instead of rules you.

Here is what you'll learn in Part III:

- **Chapter 12: Systems Beat Willpower** shows why habits succeed when goals fail, and how to set up financial systems that guarantee progress.

- **Chapter 13: Relationships, Networks, and Who You Listen To** shows how to build a circle that expands opportunities, protects you, and multiplies your wealth.

- **Chapter 14: Teaching Wealth to the Next Generation** shows how to pass down knowledge, not just dollars, so the wealth you build actually lasts.

- **Chapter 15: Your 20-Year Wealth Blueprint** shows how to pull everything together into one plan you can follow for the rest of your life.

If you do the work, Part III is where you stop thinking about survival and start building your legacy.

12.
Systems Beat Willpower

Habits make wealth automatic. Systems succeed where willpower fails.

Most people think money is about discipline. They believe if they could just "try harder," they would save more, spend less, and invest smarter. But trying harder is not a plan. Discipline fades. Motivation dies. Willpower burns out.

Think about the last time you set a New Year's resolution. Maybe you promised yourself you would budget, stop using credit cards, or finally start investing. How long did it last? A week? A month? At some point, life happened. Bills came in, stress built up, you got tired, and the resolution fell apart. That's how willpower works. It might get you started, but it'll never carry you through years or even decades.

Habits and systems are stronger than willpower. Habits take the decision-making out of your hands. They run in the background, day after day, even when you're tired or distracted. Systems lock those habits in place. Systems make saving, investing, and protecting your money happen automatically whether you feel motivated or not.

That's the difference between poor households and wealthy ones. Poor households rely on emotion. They save when they feel motivated, but the moment life gets stressful, the savings stop. They invest when the market feels safe, and they sell the moment it feels scary. They operate on feelings.

Wealthy households rely on systems. They don't wonder if they'll save this month. The transfer already happened. They don't guess if they can afford an expense. The budget already decided. They don't panic about market swings. Their investments are automated and diversified. Systems protect them from their own emotions.

This isn't about being smarter. It's about being structured. The wealthy don't wake up every morning with superhuman discipline. They wake up to systems that make discipline unnecessary.

If you want financial freedom, stop relying on willpower and start building systems. That's how wealth becomes consistent instead of accidental.

Why Habits Beat Motivation

Motivation is a sugar high. It feels powerful in the moment but crashes quickly. That's why gyms are full in January and empty in March. It's why notebooks are filled with budgets in week one and tossed in a drawer by week three. Motivation is exciting, but it doesn't last.

How many times have you made a budget, stuck to it for a week, and then abandoned it when the weekend came? How many times have you promised yourself you would start saving "next month" only to see the money disappear on bills, dinners, or impulse spending? The problem wasn't that you didn't care. The problem was that you were relying on motivation to carry you.

Habits are different. Habits don't require daily effort or inspiration. Once built, they run on autopilot. You don't wake up and think hard about brushing your teeth. You don't debate whether to shower or whether to lock your door before leaving the house. These are automatic behaviors. Wealthy people treat money the same way.

When saving and investing become habits, money flows in the right direction without a fight. The transfer to savings happens on payday, not when you "remember." Contributions to investments are automated, not debated. Bills are paid on autopilot so you never rack up late fees. The system does the work that motivation can't.

Poor households rely on energy, willpower, and the good intentions of tomorrow. Wealthy households rely on habits that repeat every day, every week, every month. The difference isn't knowledge. It's consistency. Habits build consistency because they remove the need to choose every time.

If you've ever wondered why someone making the same income as you is building wealth while you're still stuck, chances are the difference is habits. They don't make better choices in the moment. They set up systems that remove the choice altogether.

Why Systems Beat Willpower

A system is a repeatable process that removes decision-making. It turns something that feels optional into something automatic.

- A budget is a system. It tells your money where to go before it ever lands in your account.

- Automatic transfers are a system. They move money into savings or investments before you even see it.

- A monthly check-in is a system. It forces you to stop drifting and face the numbers.

- Investing every payday is a system. You don't debate whether now is a "good time." The decision was already made.

Systems succeed where willpower fails because they don't rely on daily choices. Willpower is weak. It fades when you're tired, stressed, or distracted. Systems are strong because they don't care about how you feel on any given day.

Think about diets. Someone who "tries to eat better" gives in the moment pizza shows up. Someone with a meal plan, prepped food in the fridge, and a routine grocery list eats well without thinking. That's the power of systems.

The wealthy understand this. They don't wake up each morning deciding whether to save or invest. They already made the decision once and built a system to carry it out forever. They don't fight the same battle over and over again.

Poor households operate on willpower. They say things like:

- "I'll try to save what's left at the end of the month."

- "I'll invest when I feel more comfortable."

- "I'll stick to my budget this time."

Then life happens. The car breaks down. The kids need new shoes. A vacation looks too tempting. Suddenly the plan is gone because there was no system to protect it.

Wealthy households operate on systems. The savings transfer happens automatically on payday. Investments are scheduled and recurring. Bills are paid through autopay to avoid late fees. A monthly calendar reminder ensures net worth is reviewed. Systems create consistency even when motivation is low.

The best part is that systems don't have to be complicated. They aren't about fancy spreadsheets or apps. They're about building routines that run whether you're excited about money or not. Once you put a system in place, your financial life becomes predictable. Predictability creates progress. Progress creates wealth.

The Half Rule as a System

You already know the Half Rule from Chapter 7: save half, live on half. It's simple to understand, but its real power comes from how it works as a system. The Half Rule isn't a suggestion you follow when it feels convenient. It's a structure that removes debate and makes saving automatic.

Here is how it works. Every paycheck, half of your income moves directly into savings and investments. The other half stays available for housing, food, transportation, insurance, and lifestyle. You don't sit down at the end of the month wondering what's left. You don't bargain with yourself about whether this month is "different." The transfer already happened. The system already executed the plan.

The Half Rule proves the point: systems beat willpower. Willpower says, "I will try to save this month if nothing goes wrong." Systems say, "I already saved, because the money moved automatically before I had a chance to touch it."

This is what makes it powerful. The Half Rule eliminates two of the biggest enemies of saving: excuses and timing.

- Excuses disappear because the decision is already made.

- Timing no longer matters because the system runs on payday, not after expenses.

Even if your income fluctuates, the Half Rule adapts. Half of a small paycheck is smaller, but it still gets saved. Half of a larger paycheck is bigger, and your investments grow faster. Either way, you're always living within your means and always compounding wealth in the background.

Think about what that does over a lifetime. If you save half of every paycheck for 20 years, the amount of capital you build is staggering. Because it was systemized, you never had to rely on willpower for two decades straight. You made one decision – commit to the Half Rule – and the system carried it forward year after year.

Wealthy households understand this. They don't argue with themselves about saving. They set the system once and let it run. That's how the Half Rule shifts from an idea into a lifestyle: not because you have endless discipline, but because you built a structure that makes the right choice happen automatically.

Set It and Forget It Investing
Investing doesn't work if you only do it when you feel like it. That's not a strategy. That's gambling. Gambling depends on mood, impulse, and timing. Investing depends on discipline, repetition, and consistency.

Wealthy people remove emotion from the process by investing automatically. Every paycheck, before money even has a chance to sit in a checking account, a portion is redirected into investment accounts. It doesn't wait around to compete with new gadgets, nights out, or the latest sale. It's gone before it can be spent. This is the practical definition of "pay yourself first."

Automation is what makes this possible. You set the system one time, and it continues to run whether you feel motivated or not. When you build automatic transfers, saving and investing stop being optional. They happen like clockwork.

Where should you automate?

- **401(k) or 403(b):** Employer-sponsored retirement accounts that often come with a match. That match is free money and missing it is one of the biggest mistakes employees make.

- **Roth or Traditional IRA:** Individual retirement accounts that grow tax-free or tax-deferred. Automating contributions makes sure you fill them each year instead of scrambling at the deadline.

- **Brokerage Accounts:** Flexible accounts where you can buy ETFs, index funds, and other investments. Perfect for long-term goals outside of retirement.

- **HSAs:** If you qualify, a Health Savings Account is one of the most powerful tools available. Contributions are tax-deductible, growth is tax-free, and withdrawals for medical expenses are tax-free.

The real benefit of automation is that you no longer depend on willpower or market timing. You don't ask, "Should I invest this month?" The money is already invested. You don't try to guess if the market will rise or fall next week. You keep buying consistently, which means you automatically take advantage of both highs and lows. Over time, this smooths out returns and lets compounding work at full power.

Think of it like planting a tree. If you wait until the weather feels perfect, you may never start. But if you plant a seed every month, rain or shine, you eventually have a forest. Automatic investing is how wealthy households grow their financial forest without needing constant attention.

Set it once. Let it run. Forget about it. That's how real investing works.

Monthly and Quarterly Check-Ins
Systems don't mean ignoring money. They mean controlling it with rhythm.

Monthly Check-In
Once a month, review:

- Did savings transfer correctly?
- Did investments go through?
- Any unexpected expenses?
- Is debt being paid down?

This isn't a long meeting. Ten minutes is enough.

Quarterly Check-In
Every three months, review:

- Net worth (assets minus liabilities).
- Cash flow trends (spending vs saving).
- Portfolio performance (alignment with growth, income, and preservation).
- Insurance and protection (adequacy and coverage).

Quarterly check-ins keep you on track without obsessing daily.

The Money Calendar

One of the most powerful systems is a money calendar. It makes wealth management predictable and repeatable.

Here's a sample calendar:

- **1st of the month:** Automatic savings transfer.
- **5th:** Pay credit card in full.
- **10th:** Review expenses for leaks.
- **15th:** Automatic investment into brokerage or IRA.
- **20th:** Debt payoff check-in.
- **30th:** Net worth update.

Quarterly:
- Review portfolio allocation.
- Update financial goals.
- Adjust insurance and protection.

Annually:
- Tax review and planning.
- Estate plan review.
- Big-picture strategy session.

This calendar ensures nothing slips. Don't rely on memory or motivation. Rely on a system.

➤ A complete Money Calendar worksheet is available for download in your Wealth Toolkit.

Case Studies
Stories make the difference clear. Motivation fades. Systems last.

Case 1: Kevin the Doctor
Kevin tried budgeting apps, resolutions, and short bursts of discipline. Every January he promised himself he would save more. Every spring he slid back into old habits. His entire approach depended on willpower, and willpower failed. It

didn't matter how much he earned. It mattered that he had no system guiding his financial life.

Case 2: Lisa the Realtor

Lisa's commissions were unpredictable. Some months felt abundant, others felt tight. Instead of relying on motivation, she created one rule that changed everything. Every closing triggered automatic transfers for savings and investing. She removed emotion from the equation. By the end of the year, she had more saved than she had managed in several years of trying to "be better" with money.

Case 3: James the Small Business Owner

James built a habit that kept him accountable without micromanaging. Once every quarter he recorded his net worth. He listed assets, debts, and progress in a simple spreadsheet. Over time he saw the numbers rise, even during slow periods. That quarterly ritual gave him perspective during the tough months and kept him calm during the strong ones. The system of tracking created long-term discipline.

Case 4: Maya the Office Professional

Maya automated her financial life from the beginning. She set a percentage of her paycheck to flow directly into retirement and investment accounts. Once it was set up, she rarely touched or adjusted it. Years later she looked back and realized that the system did all the heavy lifting. She didn't have to feel motivated to save. The automation handled everything.

Case 5: Daniel the IT Specialist

Daniel's income fluctuated based on projects, overtime, and contract work. To stay consistent, he created an automatic split for every deposit into his bank account. A fixed portion went to bills, another to savings and taxes, and the remainder to investments. Even during irregular months, the system kept him steady. It protected him from overspending when money was flowing and from panic when work slowed down. Over time, consistency transformed his financial life.

Why Systems Free You

Many people resist building systems because they think it will make their life rigid. They imagine spreadsheets, rules, and endless restrictions. The truth is the opposite. Systems don't restrict you. They free you.

They free you from stress. When bills are automated and savings are automatic, you're no longer lying awake at night wondering if you forgot to pay something or worrying if you saved enough this month. The decisions are already made, and the actions happen without your constant attention.

They free you from guilt. Without systems, you live in a constant tug-of-war between what you know you should do and what you actually do. Every time you overspend, you feel guilty. Every time you miss a chance to save, you feel behind. Systems erase that cycle because the right actions are locked in ahead of time.

They free you from decision fatigue. Every day you make hundreds of small choices. What to eat, what to wear, where to spend time. If you leave money on that list, you drain energy deciding whether to save, invest, or spend. Systems remove money from the daily decision pile. Once your systems are set, money runs in the background while you focus on living your life.

This is why wealthy households often appear calm about money. They are not constantly checking accounts or stressing over every purchase. Their systems are in place. Money flows where it should. Their time and energy are spent on building, creating, and enjoying life instead of fighting fires.

Building Your Personal System

Here's how to put systems into place step by step:

1. **Automate savings.** Start with the Half Rule: half of every paycheck moves into savings and investments before you touch it. Set up automatic transfers so this happens without effort.

2. **Automate investing.** Direct contributions into retirement accounts, brokerage accounts, or HSAs each month. Consistency is more powerful than size, so even small amounts matter when automated.

3. **Automate bills.** Use online bill pay to eliminate late fees, missed payments, or forgotten due dates. Build reliability into your system.

4. **Create a money calendar.** Mark specific dates for financial tasks. The 1st for reviewing income, the 5th for checking bills, the 15th for contributions, the end of each quarter for reviewing progress, and once a year for a full financial health check.

5. **Track net worth.** Net worth is the single number that captures the big picture. Create a simple spreadsheet or use a tool that shows assets minus liabilities. Update quarterly. This gives you clarity about where you are headed.

When you combine these steps, money stops being a source of chaos and becomes a source of order. You no longer live month to month, hoping things work out. You live with structure and confidence.

Action Plan: Build Your Money Calendar
Motivation fades. Willpower fails. Systems last.

Your challenge is to design your personal money calendar. Write down what happens with your money on specific days each month.

For example:

- The 1st: paycheck comes in, Half Rule savings move automatically.
- The 5th: automatic bill payments clear.
- The 10th: investment contributions process.
- The 15th: review checking balance and adjust for the rest of the month.
- The 20th: any side hustle or freelance income moves into savings.
- The 30th: review the month and check progress.

Add quarterly reviews to track your net worth and see growth over time. Add annual reviews to update insurance, adjust investments, and revisit goals.

Once your calendar is in place, money no longer depends on your daily discipline. It runs on autopilot. Bills pay themselves. Savings happen without thought. Investments keep compounding. You stop living in stress and start living in control.

Systems beat willpower. Habits beat motivation. Build your systems today, and wealth will take care of itself tomorrow.

13.
Relationships, Networks, and Who You Listen To

The people around you determine your financial future. Choose wisely or get dragged down with the wrong crowd.

Money is never just numbers on a page. It's not just a calculator problem. It's also shaped by the people you spend time with, the conversations you hear, and the habits that surround you. Your environment pushes you toward certain choices, often without you realizing it. The people in your circle are either lifting you toward wealth or keeping you trapped in poverty.

If you spend time with people who complain about money, who waste it on every impulse, who joke about being broke, you'll start to accept that as normal. You'll copy their language, adopt their habits, and repeat their mistakes.

If you spend time with people who are disciplined with money, who invest, who talk about ownership and opportunity, you'll rise to that level instead. Wealth is contagious. Poverty is contagious. Your circle decides which one you catch.

The Impact of Your Circle
You become like the people you spend the most time with. This isn't just a saying. Research shows that people's income, savings, and even debt levels tend to match those of their closest friends and family. If everyone around you is struggling financially, the odds are high that you will too.

If your closest friends eat out five nights a week, put everything on credit cards, and treat being poor as a joke, you'll fall into the same habits. You'll convince yourself it's fine to live paycheck to paycheck because that's what everyone else does.

If instead your circle talks about saving, investing, starting businesses, buying real estate, and building for the future, you absorb those ideas. You start to believe those things are possible for you. You hear strategies you never would have discovered on your own. You start to see wealth building as normal instead of unusual.

Your circle sets your baseline for what feels normal. If overspending is normal in your group, you'll overspend. If saving and investing are normal in your group, you'll save and invest. That's why wealthy people guard their networks carefully. They know relationships aren't neutral. Every relationship is either pulling you forward or holding you back.

Stop and ask yourself a hard question. Who are the five people you spend the most time with? Do they live the kind of life you want to build? Or are they reinforcing the very habits you are trying to escape?

Why Bad Money Advice Keeps You Poor

Most people who give advice mean well. The problem is that most people are poor. They're giving advice they don't even follow themselves. They're handing out ideas that sound good in the moment but keep you trapped in the long run.

Bad advice often sounds like this:

- "You only live once, buy the car."
- "Debt is normal, everyone has it."
- "The market is risky, stay away."
- "Rich people are just lucky."
- "Wait until you make more, then start saving."

These lines feel comforting. They let you off the hook. They give you permission to spend money you don't have and to push off hard decisions for another day. They let you feel like you're not falling behind because "everyone else is doing the same thing."

But this advice is poison. It locks you into the same cycle that keeps millions stuck in financial survival mode. It convinces you that wealth is impossible, that saving is pointless, and that investing is only for other people. Once you start believing that story, you stop trying. That's how poverty passes from one generation to the next.

Think about it clearly. Would you take fitness advice from someone who has never been inside a gym? Would you take relationship advice from someone who has been divorced multiple times? Then why would you take money advice from someone living paycheck to paycheck or drowning in credit card debt?

Filter every voice you let influence you. Before you follow someone's advice, ask yourself three questions:

1. Does this person actually live the results I want for myself?

2. Do they practice what they preach, or are they just repeating what they heard from someone else?

3. Are they financially independent, or are they still struggling themselves?

If the answer is no, smile politely, thank them for sharing, and move on. Don't argue. Don't debate. Just recognize that their words are not worth following. Your financial future is too important to hand over to people who can't even manage their own.

Good Networks vs Bad Networks
Not all networks are equal. Some can change your life and accelerate your wealth. Others can waste years of your time and fill your head with bad habits that hold you back.

I've been in both types of rooms. I've sat in groups that called themselves "networking events" but were really just people barely getting by, swapping business cards, venting about their struggles, and trying to sell each other products. Nobody was growing. Nobody was learning. The energy was negative, and the conversations went nowhere.

I've also been in rooms where the level of conversation was entirely different. Successful business owners discussed hiring strategies. Investors shared deal flow. Professionals made introductions that led to new opportunities. In those groups, you could feel the momentum. The environment itself raised your standards. That's the power of a good network.

The challenge is that at first glance it's not always easy to tell the difference. Both types of groups may have similar names. Both may promise "connections" and "opportunities." The difference is in the people, the energy, and the results. If you want to build wealth, you need to learn how to separate the good from the bad.

Signs of a Bad Networking Group
A bad network isn't just unhelpful. It actively drags you down. Instead of building you up, it wastes your time, drains your energy, and fills your head with the wrong mindset. Here are the warning signs:

1. **Every meeting is about sales, not growth.**
   If the agenda is always about who sold what this week, who earned a commission, or how many leads someone squeezed out of the group, that's not networking. That's a sales scoreboard. Real growth groups talk about strategy, systems, and wealth. Bad groups obsess over short-term numbers.

2. **Cringeworthy pitch sessions.**
   If everyone takes turns standing up and rattling off the same rehearsed pitch, it's not networking. It's theater. You aren't learning, collaborating, or building. You're just trapped in a cycle of recycled slogans and forced applause.

3. **Conversations stay small.**
   When the talk is about scraping for one client, closing one tiny deal, or why the economy is too hard right now, the group is stuck in survival mode. Instead of thinking bigger, everyone is focused on keeping the lights on. That energy will rub off.

4. **No accountability or real follow-through.**
    People promise introductions that never happen. They talk about "helping each other" but never show up beyond the weekly ritual. If nothing gets built outside of the room, the group is just noise.

5. **Scarcity and desperation fill the room.**
    When everyone is clinging to the same few opportunities and operating paycheck to paycheck, the culture is fear, not abundance. Spend too long in that environment, and you will start to copy it without realizing.

6. **Anyone can join.**
    If there's no filter, no real cost, and no expectation of contribution, you get a revolving door of people who aren't serious. A strong network screens for builders. Weak groups let anyone in, which is why the quality stays low.

Signs of a Good Networking Group

A good network raises your standards. It stretches you, challenges you, and exposes you to people who are further ahead on the path. Here are the signs:

1. **The room stretches you.**
    If you're always the smartest or most successful person in the room, you're not learning. In a good group, you feel like you need to rise to meet the level of conversation. That stretch makes you grow.

2. **Value exchange is real.**
    You leave with new ideas, new insights, or new introductions. Members share strategies that actually work, not just opinions. People give without expecting an immediate return because they know long-term relationships are what matter.

3. **The focus is on growth, not excuses.**
    Conversations revolve around opportunities, problem-

solving, and creative ideas. Challenges are met with solutions, not complaints. You walk away energized, not drained.

4. **Success leaves clues.**
   Members of good groups are not just talking. They are doing. They own businesses, run investments, manage portfolios, and build projects. Seeing their progress proves what is possible and gives you a model to follow.

5. **Commitment is required.**
   Good groups often cost a fair amount of money and have an application process. This isn't a bad thing. It filters for people who are serious about growth. A small investment in membership often buys access to a much larger pool of opportunities and higher-level conversations.

How to Figure Out Which Is Which

At first glance, both good and bad groups can look polished. The people may be dressed well, the event may have a nice venue, and the pitch may sound professional. That doesn't tell you the truth. To know whether a group is worth your time, you need to look deeper.

Ask yourself:

- **Did I leave with at least one new idea or introduction worth pursuing?**
  A strong group always gives you something you can act on. It may be a strategy you had not considered, an introduction to someone who can help, or a new way of thinking about your money and business. If you walk out empty-handed, the group didn't deliver value.

- **Are the people in the room living at a level I aspire to, or are they stuck at a level I want to escape?**
  Look around. Are members building businesses, managing investments, or creating opportunities? Or are they just trying to survive? If you see people who are already where you want to be, that is the right room. If you see people stuck where you started, you're wasting time.

- **Did the group feel like an investment in my future, or just a time-killer?**
  Time is the one resource you can never get back. A good group feels like an investment. Even if you spend two hours, you leave with clarity and direction. A bad group feels like a drain. You wonder why you bothered showing up.

- **Do the members talk about building wealth, or do they just trade small wins?**
  Small wins sound like bragging about one sale, one client, or one lucky break. Wealth conversations focus on systems, scale, and strategies that last. Pay attention to the language. The words people use reveal whether they are playing small or building big.

- **Do I feel pulled up, or pulled down?**
  This is the simplest test. After leaving the group, check your energy. Do you feel challenged, motivated, and stretched to grow? Or do you feel drained, skeptical, and doubtful? Your gut will tell you. If you feel pulled up, you are in the right room. If you feel pulled down, you need to leave.

The difference comes down to energy and trajectory. Bad groups keep you stuck where you are. Good groups show you what is possible and pull you forward. If you leave with clarity, confidence, and new connections, you found the right one. If you leave with excuses, complaints, or a heavier weight, you were in the wrong room.

Mini Worksheet: Room Quick Audit
After attending a networking group, reflect on these questions:

- What did I walk away with that has real value: a strategy, an introduction, or an insight I can apply right now?

- Who in the room was operating at a higher level than me, and what did I learn from them?

- How did the energy of the room affect me: did it motivate me, or did it drain me with negativity and endless pitches?

- Were the conversations centered on building businesses, portfolios, and wealth, or mostly on trading small deals and scraping commissions?

- What level of commitment was expected to be part of the group: was there a real filter for seriousness, or could anyone wander in?

- Would I feel confident inviting someone I deeply respect into this room, or would I worry about how it reflects on me?

If your reflections point toward growth, energy, and accountability, you're in a good room. If they point toward scarcity, desperation, or wasted time, it's the wrong room.

➤ The full Room Audit Worksheet is available for download in your Wealth Toolkit.

Mentors: Shortcut to Wisdom
Peers influence habits. Mentors change trajectories.

A mentor isn't just someone older or smarter. A mentor is someone who has already done what you want to do. They've walked the path, made the mistakes, and achieved results. They've built businesses, invested wisely, created wealth, and learned lessons you can't find in a textbook.

The value of a mentor is simple: they save you years. What you could figure out through trial and error in a decade, they can point out in an hour. They keep you from walking into traps that could cost you time, money, and peace of mind.

How do you find one?

- **Look in your workplace or industry.** Pay attention to people who are respected, consistent, and proven.

- **Ask for guidance from someone you respect.** You'll be surprised how many successful people are willing to share if they see you are serious.

- **Offer value in return.** Do research, make introductions, share ideas, or help with projects. Don't just take, find ways to give.

- **Be humble and teachable.** Mentors don't waste time on people who argue or defend bad habits. They invest in people who listen and act.

A mentor doesn't need to be a billionaire or a celebrity. They just need to be ahead of you in the direction you want to go. Even one good mentor can accelerate your path more than any book, class, or podcast.

Partners: Who You Build With
The wrong partner can destroy your finances. The right partner multiplies them. This is true in business and also in life.

Life Partners
If one person saves and the other spends recklessly, wealth will not grow. You'll always fight uphill battles. Financial alignment is not optional in relationships. It's survival. Talk about money early. Discuss spending, saving, debt, and goals before marriage or major commitments. The strongest couples see themselves as a team. They pull in the same direction.

A partner who supports your financial vision doubles your strength. A partner who fights it cuts it in half. Or worse.

Business Partners
Don't choose business partners based on friendship or excitement alone. Excitement fades. Values and discipline last. A good partner

shares the same vision, values, and work ethic. They bring skills that complement yours, not duplicate them.

Always use written contracts. Always define roles, responsibilities, and exit strategies. A handshake is not protection. A reckless or dishonest partner can sink everything you build. A well-chosen partner, on the other hand, can multiply your growth, share the load, and open doors you could not open alone.

Case Study: When the Wrong Partner Almost Sinks You

I went through this myself. I brought on an older financial advisor with the intent to buy his practice. On paper, it looked like the perfect fit. I invested heavily to make the merger work by expanding to a larger office space, hiring more staff, and structuring operations for a bigger combined firm.

Then, at the last minute, he decided not to sell. Just like that, the deal collapsed. I was left holding the costs of a larger office and more staff without the revenue I had built the plan around. It almost bankrupted me.

The lesson was painful but important. Never make big financial moves based on a handshake deal or someone else's intentions. Protect yourself with contracts, contingencies, and the assumption that things can fall through. A partner who isn't fully committed can cost you everything.

Case Study: The Right Partner Multiplies

I also experienced the opposite. At another stage in my career, I partnered with someone who shared my vision and values. They brought skills I didn't have, and I brought strengths that balanced theirs. We documented everything, set clear expectations, and worked with transparency.

The result was growth neither of us could have achieved alone. Because we trusted the process and held each other accountable, the business expanded faster, clients were served better, and opportunities came more easily. That partnership wasn't just about splitting work. It was about multiplying results.

The difference between the wrong partner and the right one is the difference between collapse and acceleration. Choose carefully, and a partner can become one of your greatest assets.

Strategies to Build a Strong Network

A strong network doesn't happen by accident. It's built with intention. The people you surround yourself with will either pull you up or pull you down. If you want to build wealth, you need to be deliberate about where you spend your time and who you spend it with.

1. Go where builders gather.

You won't find serious wealth builders at the bar every Friday night complaining about their jobs. You'll find them at industry meetups, investment clubs, real estate groups, entrepreneurial conferences, and professional associations. These rooms may feel intimidating at first, but that's exactly the point. Growth happens when you enter circles that stretch you.

2. Invest in events.

Free networking events often attract people who are dabbling, not building. When you pay for entry, you filter for seriousness. A $500 real estate seminar or $1,000 industry conference may feel like a cost, but it's actually an investment. One introduction, one idea, or one partnership can return that investment tenfold.

3. Start conversations.

Don't stand in the corner waiting for opportunities to come to you. Walk up to people. Ask what they are working on. Listen closely. Take genuine interest. The best way to build relationships is to show you care about others' goals, not just your own.

4. Give value first.

Most people show up asking, "What can I get?" Wealthy networkers ask, "What can I give?" Can you introduce someone to a useful contact? Share a helpful tool? Recommend a resource? The fastest way to build trust is to be generous before you expect anything back.

5. Curate your media diet.

Your "network" isn't just the people you meet in person. It's also the voices you allow into your mind every day. Social media, podcasts, YouTube channels, blogs, and even group chats shape your beliefs about money more than most people realize.

Here is the danger: Online, the loudest voices often know the least.

Influencers with no real track record present themselves as experts. Gurus promise "financial freedom" if you just buy their course. YouTube creators claim you can retire in five years with crypto, day trading, dropshipping, or some secret shortcut they conveniently sell. They show you rented cars, fake screenshots, and edited lifestyles to make you believe their story is real.

Their goal is not to make you wealthy.
Their goal is to make *themselves* wealthy by selling you the fantasy.

The psychological trap is powerful. When you watch these gurus long enough, you start believing you are "one strategy away" or "one course away" from changing everything. You start chasing shortcuts. You start comparing your real life to their fake highlight reel. That mindset is dangerous because it replaces discipline with delusion.

Most people lose money following online gurus. They jump from one "hot opportunity" to the next, never building real skills, real systems, or real wealth.

This is why **you must always do your own research.**

Don't take any financial strategy at face value because someone online "sounded smart." Scammers and hype-sellers often sound the smartest. They are trained to be persuasive. They know the words to use. They know the emotional buttons to push. They know how to make you feel like you are missing out or falling behind.

Real wealth isn't built through blind trust. It's built through understanding.

- Before you invest in anything, learn what it is.
- Before you follow someone's advice, verify their credibility.
- Before you risk your money, make sure you actually know how the strategy works.
- Protect your attention the way wealthy people protect their capital.

Replace hype voices with responsible ones. Replace influencers who sell dreams with teachers who explain reality. Follow people who talk about budgeting, investing, ownership, long-term planning, and risk management. If someone promises guaranteed returns or fast money, unfollow immediately.

Your media diet determines your mindset. Your mindset determines your actions. Your actions determine your financial future.

A strong network multiplies your opportunities. A weak network multiplies your excuses. Be intentional. The right voices accelerate everything.

The Family Factor
Family influence can be the most powerful of all. It can also be the most dangerous. Parents, siblings, or extended family often mean well, but they may pass down outdated or destructive financial ideas.

Some families normalize debt. Others believe investing is too risky. Some may discourage you from taking a new opportunity because it feels unsafe compared to "a steady job." They aren't trying to hurt you, but their mindset can keep you trapped.

You can't change your family's money habits by arguing. Arguing only creates tension. What you can do is set clear boundaries and lead by example. Respect them, but recognize that you don't need to take financial advice from relatives who are broke, drowning in debt, or constantly stressed about money.

When your aunt tells you, "Everyone has car loans, that's just life," smile and change the subject. When your cousin insists investing is gambling, nod politely and keep investing. You don't have to fight every battle.

Over time, results speak louder than arguments. When your emergency fund covers a crisis without stress, they'll notice. When your investments start producing income, they'll notice. When you live debt-free, they'll notice. At first, they may mock or discourage you. Later, they may quietly ask how you did it.

Family shapes your early beliefs about money, but as an adult, you choose which beliefs you keep. Take the good values like hard work, resilience, and gratitude. Leave behind the ones that keep you poor.

Case Studies

Case 1: The Drag — Maya's Wake-Up Call

Maya used to spend her weekends with a group of coworkers who lived for brunch, shopping trips, and impulsive getaways. No one saved. No one invested. Everyone joked about being "broke together," as if it were a personality trait instead of a problem.

Maya unconsciously matched their habits because she wanted to fit in. Her savings never grew. Her credit card balances did. Every time she thought about getting serious with money, her circle brushed it off. They encouraged fun, not discipline, and she absorbed their mindset without realizing it.

One day, Maya attended an investing workshop at her local community center. The room felt different. People were talking about budgeting systems, long-term planning, and building assets. The conversations opened her eyes to how much her environment had shaped her thinking.

Slowly, she spent less time with her old group and more time learning from people who were building something real. Two years later, she was saving consistently, investing automatically, and building real traction. It started with choosing a different room.

Case 2: The Mentor — Daniel's Turning Point

Daniel always chased the next big thing: crypto, options, speculative tech plays. He followed online gurus who promised fast money, but the results were always the same. Huge excitement. Big gains. Bigger losses. He felt stuck repeating the same cycle.

Everything shifted when Daniel met an experienced IT manager who had quietly built wealth through diversification and long-term investing. Instead of hype, the mentor talked about systems, patience, and risk management. Daniel asked questions, listened, and offered help whenever possible. He never asked for shortcuts because he finally understood they didn't exist.

Over time, the mentor showed him how to build a real plan, not a string of guesses. Daniel learned to automate savings, stop gambling, and invest for the future. His results changed because his source of advice changed. One mentor replaced years of noise and turned confusion into clarity.

Case 3: The Partner — James Learns the Hard Way

James always wanted to expand beyond his small business, and when a friend approached him with a "can't lose" idea, he agreed immediately. What he ignored was the friend's lack of discipline: no budgeting, no contracts, no tracking, and no accountability.

The business collapsed within two years. Bills piled up. Savings disappeared. James was left to clean up the mess alone. It nearly broke him.

But it also taught him what to look for. Years later, he partnered with someone who had steady habits and complementary strengths. They drafted formal agreements, set clear expectations, and kept finances transparent. That partnership grew into a stable, profitable business because it was built on discipline rather than enthusiasm.

The difference between failure and success wasn't the idea. It was the partner.

Case 4: Two Rooms — Lisa's Networking Shift

As a realtor, Lisa attended every free networking group she could find. Many of them looked polished at first, but the meetings were always the same. People complaining about slow markets. Members taking turns pitching their services. Endless talk about sales commissions instead of real growth. She left feeling drained and uninspired.

Then she paid to join a private professional group filled with business owners, investors, and entrepreneurs who were actively building wealth. The conversations were elevated. People shared strategies, numbers, and lessons from both wins and failures. Members opened doors instead of just asking for referrals.

Within months, Lisa gained new clients, learned smarter business systems, and received guidance that helped her shift from a commission-chasing mindset to an ownership mindset. The free groups cost her time. The right group multiplied her results.

The room you choose determines the opportunities you receive. Lisa stepped into a better room, and everything changed.

The Network Roadmap

Stage 1 (0–6 months):
- Audit your circle. Identify negative and positive influences.
- Limit exposure to toxic advice.
- Follow three new responsible voices online.

Stage 2 (6–18 months):
- Join a professional or investment group.
- Attend one live event.
- Add one financially responsible peer to your circle.

Stage 3 (18–36 months):
- Find and approach a mentor.
- Join or form a mastermind for accountability.
- Replace one negative influence with a positive one.

Action Plan: Replace One Negative with One Positive

Wealth is contagious. Poverty is contagious too. The people closest to you will either lift you up or pull you down. You can't always control who's in your life, but you can control how much influence they have over your financial future.

Your challenge: replace one negative influence with one positive. If you have a friend who constantly complains about money and discourages you from trying new things, limit your time with them. If you have a relative who insists that "debt is normal" or "investing is risky," stop letting their fears dictate your choices. You don't need to cut them out of your life completely, but you do need to cut their influence over your decisions.

Then, intentionally add one positive force. This could be a peer who's building wealth, a mentor who has already achieved what you want, or a group of people who think bigger than you currently do. It could even be a virtual community, a mastermind, or a podcast that fills your head with the right voices. One strong positive connection can outweigh several negative ones.

Think about it this way: every conversation is either planting weeds or planting seeds. Weeds choke progress. Seeds grow into opportunities. Replace one source of weeds with one source of seeds, and you immediately change the environment you're growing in.

Start small. Find one person, one group, or one resource that challenges you to level up. Over time, those choices stack up. A new circle creates new habits. New habits create new opportunities. And those opportunities create a new financial reality.

Your circle will shape your future whether you choose it carefully or not. Don't leave it to chance. Choose wisely and choose today.

14.
Teaching Wealth to the Next Generation

Break the cycle. Give your children the tools you never had and change your family's future forever.

Money mistakes aren't just individual. They're generational. Families pass down beliefs about money in the same way they pass down recipes, traditions, and habits. If your parents were poor with money, there's a good chance you inherited their habits without even realizing it.

That cycle can stop with you.

Financial literacy isn't taught in most schools. Children won't learn about compounding, debt traps, or wealth-building portfolios from textbooks. They might learn how to calculate the slope of a line or memorize the periodic table, but they'll graduate without knowing how to balance a budget or build credit responsibly.

If you want your children to live differently, you need to teach them differently. You must give them the tools you never had. When you do, you change the future of your family. You break the cycle of generational poverty and create a foundation of generational wealth.

Why Financial Literacy Must Start at Home
Think about how most children learn about money. They see parents swipe cards, argue about bills, avoid phone calls from creditors, or say things like "we can't afford that." Rarely do they see saving systems, investing habits, or calm planning around money.

Schools aren't filling the gap. A growing number of states require financial literacy courses, but most programs are shallow. They cover surface-level ideas about checking accounts and debt, but they don't teach students how to invest, how to build multiple streams of income, or how to avoid lifestyle creep.

Cycles of financial struggle repeat because beliefs and habits are inherited. Children grow up absorbing the behaviors they see. Poor families pass down survival habits: spend what you earn, use debt to cover the rest, and hope the future takes care of itself. Wealthy families pass down ownership habits: live below your means, invest consistently, protect assets, and grow systems that work long after you stop.

If you want your children to become owners rather than consumers, you can't wait for a teacher or a course. The lessons need to begin at home.

Breaking the Silence
Many parents avoid talking about money with their kids. They think it's too complicated, too stressful, or inappropriate for children to understand. But silence teaches too. Silence teaches that money is shameful, secretive, or off-limits. That silence is exactly why so many young adults graduate with no idea how to handle real financial life.

You don't need to share every detail of your net worth or investments with young children, but you must normalize money conversations. Start simple and expand as they grow. Treat money as a tool that can be understood, managed, and mastered. If they learn this early, they won't fear money later.

Teaching Kids About Saving
Saving comes first. Kids need to learn how to set money aside intentionally before they can put it to work.

Start Small and Make It Visible
Even young children can learn about saving. Give them three jars or envelopes labeled Spend, Save, and Give. Every time they receive money from chores, allowance, or gifts, have them divide it into those categories. The physical act of putting money aside creates a connection in their brain that digital swipes can't.

Match Their Savings
Encourage saving by matching what they put aside. If your child saves $5, add another $5. This creates a sense of reward and mirrors

how employers match contributions in retirement accounts. They'll learn that saving attracts rewards.

Teach Delayed Gratification
Saving is ultimately about patience. If they want a toy, encourage them to save up and buy it themselves. The wait teaches discipline and proves that saving leads to bigger rewards. Delayed gratification is one of the most important traits of wealthy people.

Teaching Kids About Investing
Saving isn't enough. Kids need to learn that money grows when it's invested.

Ownership Lessons
Explain that investing is owning. If your child loves a brand, show them how to buy one share of that company. If they love Netflix, show them what it means to own Netflix stock. Connect their world to ownership so they understand investing is not abstract.

Compounding Lessons
Show them how money grows. Use simple examples. If they invest $100 and earn 10 percent, next year they have $110. If that $110 earns another 10 percent, they have $121. This simple lesson shows the snowball effect of compounding.

Custodial Accounts
Open a custodial investment account. Contribute small amounts consistently, ideally their own money that they've earned. Let them watch it grow over time. When they see their account balance rise, the lesson will stick in a way lectures never could.

Teaching Kids About Entrepreneurship
Entrepreneurship teaches responsibility, creativity, and ownership. It proves that money can be created, not just earned.

Encourage small ventures:
- Lemonade stands or bake sales.
- Babysitting or lawn care.

- Selling handmade crafts online.
- Starting a YouTube channel or digital store.

The goal is not immediate profit. The goal is experience. Let them learn what it feels like to have an idea, set a price, and serve a customer.

Ask guiding questions:
- What problem are you solving?
- Who is your customer?
- How much does it cost to deliver your product or service?
- How will you let people know about it?

These simple conversations help build entrepreneurial muscles.

Breaking Cycles of Generational Poverty
Generational poverty isn't only a lack of money. It's a set of inherited beliefs and habits that get passed from parent to child without anyone realizing it is happening.

Common beliefs in poor families include:
- Debt is normal.
- Rich people are greedy or dishonest.
- Money is stressful and dangerous.
- We just aren't good with money.
- We can't afford things and there's nothing we can do about it.

These beliefs trap families in cycles of financial struggle.

To break the cycle, you must replace them with new beliefs:
- Debt is toxic and should be eliminated.
- Wealthy people are often creators and problem-solvers.
- Money is a tool that creates stability and opportunity.
- Our family builds, invests, and grows.
- We don't say "We can't afford it." We say "We choose to spend our money in ways that support our goals."

That last shift matters more than most parents realize. When children hear "We can't afford it," they internalize scarcity thinking. When they hear "We choose not to spend money on that," they learn that money is about decisions, not limitations. It teaches control, discipline, and intentionality instead of fear.

Children who grow up in a home where wealth is discussed positively, where saving and investing are visible, and where smart money choices are framed as choices, break free from poverty thinking. They learn that wealth is built by design, not by chance.

Teaching Through Modeling

Children learn more from what you do than what you say. They copy habits.

- If you save, they learn saving is normal.
- If you invest, they learn investing is normal.
- If you budget, they learn money has a plan.
- If you stay calm about money, they learn money can be controlled.

Involve them in age-appropriate ways. Let them see you pay bills, contribute to investments, and discuss financial decisions calmly. Show them that money is something to be managed, not feared.

Common Mistakes Parents Make

Parents often want the best for their children, but when it comes to money, even good intentions can create bad results. These are the mistakes that keep families trapped in cycles of confusion, stress, and poor habits.

1. **Silence**
   Not talking about money leaves kids clueless. Children learn by observation. If you never explain how bills are paid, how saving works, or how credit cards can hurt, they'll leave home without tools. Silence guarantees they repeat the same mistakes you made, only with higher costs and fewer excuses.

2. **Hypocrisy**

   Telling kids to save while you overspend destroys credibility. Kids notice everything. If you lecture them about saving but keep buying gadgets, cars, or eating out daily, they'll ignore your words and follow your actions. Kids don't learn what you say. They learn what you do.

3. **Handouts**

   Giving everything without teaching responsibility creates entitlement. When kids never earn money or manage money, they grow up expecting wealth without effort. That entitlement becomes dangerous in adulthood, where no one hands them free paychecks. Teaching responsibility means giving opportunities to earn, not endless gifts.

4. **Shame**

   Making money a negative or stressful topic creates fear. Some households treat money as taboo, only discussing it during fights or moments of crisis. This teaches kids that money equals stress. They grow up afraid of it, avoiding financial planning until problems force them into it.

5. **Overcomplication**

   Kids need simple, practical lessons, not lectures filled with jargon. Talking about "compound annual growth rates" means nothing to a child. But showing how a $10 bill grows if you save and invest it does. Simple lessons stick. Complex lectures confuse.

The Generational Wealth Roadmap

Generational wealth isn't just about leaving money behind. It's about passing down **habits, systems, and knowledge** that ensure the next generation continues to grow what you built rather than lose it. Money disappears when skills disappear. Wealth lasts when the principles behind it are taught clearly and early.

Here's the roadmap for creating financially capable children and financially strong families, organized by age and life stage.

Stage 1: Young Kids (Ages 5–10) – Foundations
At this age, money lessons must be simple, visual, and consistent.

Core goals:
- Build basic awareness
- Teach patience and choices
- Introduce the idea of ownership

Strategies:
- Use Spend, Save, and Give jars so children see money flow instead of abstract numbers.
- Teach delayed gratification by encouraging them to save for a toy rather than buying impulse treats.
- Show that money is a tool by letting them decide how to allocate small amounts.
- Connect brands they recognize to companies to introduce the idea of investing

These early lessons create emotional comfort with money. Kids who learn these basics grow into adults who don't fear money or avoid talking about it.

Stage 2: Teen Years (Ages 11–15) – Expansion
This is the perfect window to teach real skills without overwhelming them.

Core goals:
- Build confidence with real accounts
- Introduce the Half Rule
- Encourage entrepreneurship

Strategies:
- Help them open a savings account and show them how deposits grow over time.
- Introduce the Half Rule using their allowance or income from chores.

- Open a custodial brokerage account and let them invest small amounts in broad index funds.
- Encourage small business activities like mowing lawns, tutoring, pet sitting, or selling items online.
- Begin involving them in simple discussions about the family budget so they see how adults manage money.

Kids who learn these skills develop financial identity early. They begin to see themselves as earners, savers, and owners.

Stage 3: Young Adults (Ages 16–20) – Independence
This stage determines whether they thrive or struggle when they leave home.

Core goals:
- Build responsibility
- Teach real-world money systems
- Establish investing habits early

Strategies:
- Open a custodial Roth IRA if they have earned income so they see the power of compounding.
- Teach them how credit works, how scores are built, and why debt traps people.
- Let them manage part of their real expenses such as gas, clothes, or extracurricular costs.
- Encourage them to take on larger entrepreneurial projects that teach leadership and risk.
- Walk them through their first paychecks and show how taxes, withholdings, and benefits work.

By the end of this stage, they should understand the basics of income, credit, expenses, and the importance of investing early.

Stage 4: Launch (Ages 21+) – Adult Wealth Building
This stage builds the habits that carry them through the rest of their financial life.

Core goals:
- Teach real investing
- Deepen money systems
- Build multiple income streams

Strategies:
- Teach them how a portfolio actually works: stocks, bonds, ETFs, allocation, and rebalancing.
- Show them how the Half Rule accelerates independence and how automatic investing creates momentum.
- Teach basic tax planning so they understand why Roth accounts, HSAs, and 401(k) matches matter.
- Encourage them to start building additional income streams early instead of waiting until later in life.

Young adults who learn this stage early leap ahead of their peers by an entire decade.

Stage 5: Legacy Stage – Passing Down Systems, Not Just Money

Wealth is lost when families only pass down money. It survives when they pass down systems, discipline, and responsibility.

Core goals:
- Transfer knowledge
- Protect assets
- Build a financial culture

Strategies:
- Teach them the foundational systems: the Half Rule, emergency funds, automatic investing, and consistent tracking.
- Introduce them to protection strategies like insurance, wills, trusts, and LLCs so they understand how wealth is guarded.
- Hold regular family conversations about money, goals, and long-term planning so open communication becomes normal.

- Encourage each generation to teach the next, creating a self-reinforcing cycle of financial competency.

Generational wealth isn't just about leaving dollars. It's about leaving a blueprint that future generations know how to use.

➤ The full Family Wealth Lesson Plan (full age-by-age grid) is available for download in your Wealth Toolkit.

Action Plan: Teach One Wealth Lesson This Week
Generational change does not start with a massive trust fund. It begins with one simple lesson.

Your challenge this week is to teach your child one wealth principle. Show them how saving works by putting money in a jar. Explain compounding by showing them how money grows in an account. Walk them through how credit cards trap people. Or simply share how you invest or how you budget.

Don't wait for schools to teach it. Don't assume kids will figure it out later. Schools may never cover it, and "later" is often too late. The future of your family depends on what you pass down. Break the cycle you inherited. Build a better one for the next generation.

15.

Your 20-Year Wealth Blueprint

Wealth isn't built overnight. Follow this roadmap for every decade of your life and watch it multiply.

Wealth isn't built overnight. It's built brick by brick, day by day, year by year, and decade by decade. The challenge is that most people drift through life with no real plan. They live in reaction mode. They react to bills when they arrive. They react to debt when it becomes unmanageable. They react to emergencies only after they strike. By the time they finally stop to think about the future, twenty or thirty years have already passed, and there's little to show for it.

If you want a different outcome, you need to live by design instead of reaction. You need a plan that stretches across decades, not just months. A long-term wealth blueprint that gives you direction even when the unexpected happens. Not vague dreams or motivational quotes, but a concrete framework that keeps you on track.

This is that blueprint. It'll show you how to build, protect, and multiply wealth over the next twenty years, with milestones to hit along the way.

The Power of Thinking in Decades
Most people think in short cycles. They worry about paying this month's bills, getting through the week, or planning the next vacation. Wealthy people think differently. They think in decades. They measure decisions not by how they feel in the moment, but by how they'll look years from now.

They ask themselves questions like:

- What will this investment be worth in twenty years if I let compounding work?

- How will this decision affect not just me, but my children and grandchildren?

- If I build the right systems today, how much freedom will they give me later?

- Will this purchase add value to my life long-term, or will it be forgotten in a few months?

This shift in perspective changes everything. When you zoom out and start thinking in decades, short-term noise loses its power. Market crashes look smaller. Recessions look temporary. A bad month or even a bad year becomes just one page in a much larger book. You stop chasing quick wins and start building lasting wealth.

Your 20-year blueprint is not about perfection. It's about direction. If you follow it decade by decade, even imperfectly, you'll still arrive at a place most people never reach: financial freedom, independence from paychecks, and the ability to pass on a real legacy.

Your 20s: Build the Foundation
Your 20s aren't about being rich. They're about building the habits and avoiding the traps that will determine the rest of your life.

1. Build Habits
The most important thing in your 20s isn't income, it's habits. Automate savings. Start investing early, even if it's small. Learn to live on less than you earn. These habits compound far more than money.

2. Avoid Debt Traps
Credit cards, payday loans, buy-now-pay-later, car loans… These are traps designed to enslave young adults. If you avoid bad debt in your 20s, you're already ahead of 90 percent of your peers.

3. Start Investing
Don't wait until you are "making more." Start now. Even $100 a month matters. Open a Roth IRA if you qualify. Begin ownership early so compounding has time to work.

4. Learn Skills

Your 20s are for skill acquisition. Learn skills that multiply income: sales, communication, leadership, finance, technology. These skills pay dividends forever.

5. Experiment, But Learn

Your 20s are the time to try businesses, side hustles, and careers. If you fail, learn and move on. The biggest mistake is not trying.

Your 30s: Build and Grow

Your 30s are about turning habits into real wealth. You're no longer experimenting. You're building.

1. Grow Income

Use the skills you learned in your 20s to grow your income. Ask for raises, change jobs strategically, or build a business. Higher income accelerates wealth if you keep expenses controlled.

2. Family Planning

If you start a family, build systems early. Life insurance, wills, and savings accounts for children. Teach kids about money. Don't let family expenses become an excuse for financial chaos.

3. Buy Assets, Not Liabilities

Most people in their 30s stretch for a bigger house and nicer car. Instead, focus on assets: rental properties, businesses, and portfolios. Assets feed you. Liabilities drain you.

4. Solidify Systems

Budgeting, automatic investing, and debt payoff should be ingrained by now. If they aren't, fix them. Your 30s are your chance to lock systems in place before expenses grow larger.

Your 40s: Scale and Protect

By your 40s, you should be scaling wealth and protecting what you have built. This is the decade where most people plateau or lose momentum. You can't afford to coast.

1. Scale Wealth
Increase investments aggressively. Use extra income to acquire more assets. Add real estate, expand businesses, and push portfolios higher.

2. Protect Assets
Insurance, trusts, and legal structures become critical. You can't afford to lose what you've built. Add umbrella insurance, LLCs for businesses, and estate planning.

3. Legacy Thinking
Start thinking about legacy. Teach your children about investing. Involve them in financial discussions. Begin planning how wealth will transfer smoothly.

4. Avoid Midlife Debt
Many people in their 40s fall into midlife debt from lifestyle creep: new cars, expensive vacations, private schools. These can destroy momentum. Stay disciplined.

Your 50s and Beyond: Freedom and Succession
Your 50s and later decades are about preparing for freedom, succession, and legacy. This is where the blueprint really pays off.

1. Retirement Preparation
This doesn't mean stopping work. It means having the freedom to stop if you want to. Review retirement accounts, Social Security, and cash flow. Ensure investments generate income streams.

2. Succession Planning
If you own businesses or properties, create clear succession plans. Don't leave your family scrambling if something happens. Use trusts, wills, and buy-sell agreements.

3. Teaching Others
By now you should not only be financially secure, you should be teaching the next generation. Share your systems with children and grandchildren. Build a family culture around wealth.

4. Guard Against Complacency
Even in later years, avoid complacency. Inflation, taxes, and poor decisions can still erode wealth. Stay active, stay disciplined, and continue reviewing systems.

Case Studies
Case 1: The Drifter
Emily entered adulthood with decent income but no structure at all. Money came in and money went out without purpose. She upgraded apartments every few years, financed cars she could not truly afford, and used credit cards as if they were extra income. Her friends looked successful, so she spent more to keep up with them, even though they were struggling too.

In her thirties, her expenses kept growing but her savings didn't. By her forties, she was juggling debt payments, refinancing past mistakes, and hoping each tax refund would solve her problems. Every financial choice she made was emotional or reactive. She had no automatic savings, no investments, and no long-term strategy.

By her fifties, she had almost nothing to show for thirty years of work. No assets. No cushion. No real options. She was not poor because of her income. She was poor because she never built a system. Without a plan, time silently works against you, and it did.

Key Concept: Drifting is one of the most expensive lifestyles a person can choose.

Case 2: The Builder

James started with average income and a focused mindset. He committed early to a simple rule: pay himself first. Twenty percent of every paycheck went into savings and index funds long before he understood advanced wealth strategies. He avoided lifestyle creep and used every raise to increase savings instead of spending.

By his mid-thirties, these habits created real momentum. He had enough capital to buy a small rental property. It was not luxurious, but it produced steady cash flow. That one step opened new opportunities. Over time, he added more properties, received better financing, and eventually launched a small business tied to his industry.

By 45, James had income from three sources. His job. His real estate. His business. By 55, work had become optional. He did not stumble into wealth. He built it through discipline and structure.

Key Concept: You don't need high income. You need high consistency.

Case 3: The Cycle Breaker

Maria grew up in survival mode. Money created stress, arguments, and constant fear. She could have repeated the same patterns, but she made a decision that the cycle would stop with her.

Her twenties were not glamorous. She saved small amounts, stayed out of credit traps, and learned how money really works. She bought her first index fund with fifty dollars. She prioritized stability first, building an emergency cushion, setting up automatic savings, and paying off small debts one at a time.

Maria's greatest achievement wasn't her own financial growth. It was what she taught her children. She opened accounts for them, explained compounding, and involved them in basic financial decisions. By the time they reached adulthood, they already had savings, investments, and financial confidence.

By her fifties, Maria had secured her independence, and her children were progressing even faster. She didn't just change her own path. She changed her entire family tree.

Key Concept: Passing on knowledge is often more valuable than passing on money.

Case 4: The Late Starter
Robert ignored financial planning for decades. He earned a strong income but spent freely. At 45, he had minimal savings, high-interest debt, and a growing fear that he was too far behind.

He decided that late was still better than never. He built a strict budget, eliminated credit cards, and adopted the Half Rule. He lived on half of his income and invested the rest. It required sacrifice, but the progress was undeniable. Debt disappeared. Savings increased. He bought two rental properties by his early fifties. His investment accounts crossed seven figures before 55.

Robert didn't try to catch up by doing what everyone else was doing. He caught up by doing what almost no one is willing to do. He made wealth his main priority and acted with urgency.

Key Concept: Starting late is not the problem. Staying late is.

Comparison Table

Case	Starting Point	Key Habits/Choices	Outcome by Mid-50s	Lesson Learned
Emily, The Drifter	Decent income with no plan and high lifestyle spending	Emotional decisions, debt dependence, no system	No savings, no investments, and no financial stability	If you don't build a plan, time will work against you
James, The Builder	Average income with early discipline	Saving 20 percent, consistent investing, real estate growth, business creation	Multiple income streams and work optional by mid-50s	Consistency creates independence
Maria, The Cycle Breaker	Poverty background with no money education	Small savings, avoided debt, invested early, taught children	Broke generational patterns and accelerated her children's wealth	Knowledge compounds faster than money
Robert, The Late Starter	Midlife debt with minimal savings	Strict budget, Half Rule, aggressive investing	Seven-figure net worth and rental properties	Late is still possible with strong urgency

The Wealth Blueprint Roadmap

20s: Foundation
- Build saving and investing habits.
- Avoid debt traps.
- Learn skills that grow income.
- Experiment with entrepreneurship.

30s: Building
- Grow income.
- Start a family with financial systems.
- Buy assets, not liabilities.
- Strengthen savings and investing systems.

40s: Scaling and Protecting

- Scale investments and income streams.
- Protect with insurance and legal structures.
- Think about legacy.
- Avoid lifestyle traps.

50s+: Freedom and Succession
- Prepare retirement and succession plans.
- Focus on teaching and legacy.
- Stay active in managing wealth.
- Guard against erosion by inflation and taxes.

What If You're Starting Late?
Not everyone reading this is in their 20s with a clean slate. Many of you are in your 30s, 40s, 50s, or older and you already feel behind. You look at the earlier roadmap and think, *I missed my chance.*

You didn't. But the strategy changes.

The truth is that starting late requires sacrifice. If you're behind, you can't keep living like everyone else and expect to catch up. You have to live leaner, save more aggressively, and cut out distractions. It'll feel uncomfortable, because it's supposed to.

Think about fitness. Losing weight and building muscle is much harder at 45 than it is at 25. Your metabolism is slower, your recovery time is longer, and the bad habits you built in your 20s have stuck with you. But people still do it every single day. They change their diet, they train harder, and they stay disciplined. It takes more focus and more effort than it would have if they started younger, but it still works.

Wealth works the same way. If you're starting in your 30s, 40s, or 50s, you'll have to push harder than someone who began in their 20s. You may not have the same compounding advantage. But if you commit, you can still build real financial stability and even long-term wealth.

Starting in Your 30s

If you drifted through your 20s without saving or investing, now is the time to stop. You can't waste another decade. Cut out bad debt aggressively. Build an emergency fund. Set up automatic investing and push more into assets than your peers. You'll need to sacrifice luxuries that others in your income bracket may be enjoying. Vacations, expensive cars, eating out every week… These will need to be cut back until your foundation is secure.

Focus on income growth. Use your 30s to make bold career moves, add side hustles, or start a business. You still have compounding on your side if you begin now, but you can't wait for a "better time."

Starting in Your 40s
By your 40s, time is no longer an ally. You still have two decades of earning potential, but you need urgency.

- Slash expenses and apply the Half Rule as soon as you can.

- Max out retirement accounts: both employer-sponsored plans and IRAs.

- Add cash flow assets such as rental property or dividend-paying funds.

- Protect what you have with insurance and legal structures.

This is the decade where many of your peers give in to lifestyle creep, buying bigger houses, upgrading cars, and spending on things that don't build wealth. If you're behind, you can't afford that path. Sacrifice now gives you options later.

Think about fitness again. In your 40s, losing 20 pounds of fat is still possible, but it takes a level of focus that casual dieting can't deliver. You need discipline, consistency, and patience. The same is true with money.

Starting in Your 50s and Beyond

If you're in your 50s and starting from near zero, the window is smaller, but it is not closed.

- Focus on maximizing income: extend your career, build consulting income, or start a side business.

- Live lean. A stripped-down lifestyle allows even modest savings to go further.

- Maximize catch-up contributions to retirement accounts.

- Prioritize low-risk, income-producing assets to stabilize cash flow.

- Protect what you build with estate planning and insurance.

You may not become wealthy in the way a 25-year-old could over 40 years of compounding, but you can still build stability, reduce stress, and change your family's trajectory. You can still leave a foundation your children can build on.

Just like someone over 50 can lose weight and improve their health, you can also improve your finances. It'll take more discipline and consistency than it would have twenty years ago, but it's absolutely possible.

The Key Principle: Start Where You Are
It doesn't matter if you are 25, 45, or 65. The best time to start was yesterday. The second-best time is today.

You can't change lost time, but you can stop losing more. Build the habits now. Save aggressively. Invest consistently. Protect your wealth. Teach your children. Whether you have twenty years or five years, you can move forward instead of staying stuck.

If you're behind, accept the truth. It'll take sacrifice. You can't live like everyone else if you want different results. But the reward is freedom, stability, and the chance to rewrite your financial future.

Action Plan: Write Your One-Page Wealth Plan

Your challenge is to create a one-page wealth plan. Not a 50-page binder you will never look at again. One page. Simple, clear, and powerful.

Take a blank sheet of paper and map out the next 20 years of your life. Break it into two decades. For each decade, write down one to three priorities that matter most. In your 20s or 30s that may mean eliminating debt, building an emergency fund, and investing consistently. In your 40s and 50s that may mean growing multiple income streams, protecting assets, and teaching your family what you have learned. Keep it simple. If you can't explain it in a sentence, it is too complicated.

This one-page plan is your personal blueprint. It's your compass when life gets noisy. Review it once a year. Make adjustments as your career, family, and opportunities evolve. The plan should bend with your life, not break.

Wealth isn't built overnight. It's built brick by brick, habit by habit, year by year. The one-page plan keeps you anchored in that truth. If you follow it with consistency, you won't just create financial freedom for yourself. You'll also build a foundation that your children and grandchildren can stand on.

Legacy doesn't happen by accident. It's designed. Your one-page wealth plan is where that design begins.

Mini Worksheet: One-Page Plan Starter

Write one priority for your current decade:

- 20s: _____
- 30s: _____
- 40s: _____
- 50s+: _____

➤ The full One-Page Wealth Plan Template is available for download in your Wealth Toolkit.

Conclusion: Why You're Still Poor – And What To Do About It

If you made it this far, you already know more about money than most people will ever learn in their lifetime. You know why people stay poor. You know the myths that trap them, the habits that drain them, and the systems they ignore. You know how they sabotage their future by believing lies, by borrowing for things that do not produce income, by spending more than they earn, and by drifting through decades without a plan.

The truth has been laid bare. Wealth is not an accident. Poverty is not an accident. They are both the result of choices repeated over time. People stay poor because they accept "normal" as unchangeable. They believe debt is just part of life. They confuse consumption with success. They ignore the hidden enemies of wealth like inflation, taxes, lawsuits, and time. Most of all, they never take action.

But you now know the way out. You know how to rewire your mindset so you stop thinking like a consumer and start thinking like an owner. You know how to build systems that control cash flow automatically so you're not dependent on fleeting bursts of motivation. You know how to use the Half Rule to save and invest at a level that compresses decades of struggle into years of progress. You know how to invest in ownership instead of gambling. You know how to create multiple streams of income so that no single paycheck controls your future. You know how to protect what you build with insurance, legal structures, estate planning, and tax strategies. You know how to teach your children the lessons you were never taught so the cycle is broken forever.

That's the formula. It's direct, proven, and powerful. It's not complicated. It's not mysterious. But it's not easy.

Why Most People Won't Do It
Most people won't act. They'll read books, nod along, underline key phrases, and feel a burst of motivation that fades in a week. They'll say things like, "I'll start next month," or "I just need a little more income first." They'll wait for the perfect moment, the perfect job, the perfect investment, or the perfect conditions that never come. They'll stay in the cycle because it feels comfortable, even as it slowly drains them.

Don't be most people.

The line between poor and wealthy isn't knowledge. The difference is execution. Wealthy people don't wait for permission. They don't wait for the economy to improve. They don't wait until they feel "ready." They just act.

Why You Can
You may believe you're too far behind. You may believe your mistakes are too heavy. You may believe you need a massive income just to begin. None of those beliefs are true.

Wealth is not built by perfect people. It's built by persistent people. It's built by those who start where they are, with what they have, and refuse to quit. Even the smallest action creates a new trajectory. Paying off one toxic debt changes your future. Saving a small percentage consistently reshapes your habits. Creating one extra stream of income gives you resilience. Protecting what you build shields you from collapse.

Don't underestimate the power of starting. Starting is the hardest step. Once you put systems in motion, they begin to carry you forward. Momentum becomes your ally.

Legacy Thinking

The choices you make don't only affect you. They ripple through generations. If you apply what you learned here, you'll not just change your own life, you'll change your family tree. Your children will grow up in a home where money is not chaos, but calm. They'll see saving, investing, and entrepreneurship as normal, not strange. They'll inherit not just money, but wisdom. Wisdom lasts longer than money.

Generational poverty is real. Entire families live and die in cycles of scarcity because no one ever broke the chain. But generational wealth is just as real. Families who plant the right seeds create a harvest that lasts for centuries. You have the power to choose which one your family will experience.

Your Next Step

This book has given you the framework. You've studied the myths, the traps, the systems, and the blueprint. But knowledge alone will not save you. Information without action is useless.

Here are your assignments: Write your one-page wealth plan. Review the lessons and choose one to implement this week. Build your money calendar so your systems run on autopilot. Audit your network and replace one negative influence with one positive. Teach one lesson to your children so the next generation does not repeat the mistakes of the last. Protect what you build so one lawsuit or tax bill can't undo years of progress.

Don't wait for tomorrow. Don't wait for the next paycheck. Don't wait until you feel ready. Start now.

Final Word

Why are most people still poor? Because they believe lies. Because they let bad habits run their lives. Because they drift without systems. Because they refuse to act.

What can you do about it? Everything you just read.

You now hold the tools. You hold the roadmap. You hold the choice. There are no more excuses.

Wealth isn't about luck. It's about ownership, systems, and time. It's about persistence when others give up. If you act, you'll not only build freedom for yourself, you'll change the direction of your family forever.

That's the decision in front of you. Stay poor, or build wealth.

Choose wealth.

Sources & References

Sources

1. LendingClub & PYMNTS, *Reality Check: Paycheck-to-Paycheck Report*, 2023.
2. Federal Reserve Bank of New York, *Household Debt and Credit Report*, Q1 2024.
3. Experian, *State of Credit 2024*.
4. Bankrate, *Emergency Savings Survey*, 2023.
5. NYU Stern, *Historical Returns on Stocks, Bonds, and Bills*, updated 2023.
6. CNBC reporting, *Crypto Market Lost $2 Trillion in 2022*, Dec 2022.
7. Kiplinger, *Survey: Americans' Beliefs About Real Estate*, 2022.
8. National Endowment for Financial Education, *Lottery Winners and Bankruptcy Statistics*.
9. Forbes, *What Is Lifestyle Inflation?* 2023.
10. Bank of America, *High Earners Living Paycheck to Paycheck*, 2023.
11. PYMNTS, *High-Income Earners and Financial Stress*, 2022.
12. American Psychological Association, *Hedonic Adaptation and Consumer Behavior*, 2021.
13. Federal Reserve, *Consumer Credit – G.19 Report*, 2023.
14. Consumer Financial Protection Bureau, *Payday Lending Report*, 2022.
15. NerdWallet, *Household Credit Card Debt Study*, 2023.
16. Gallup, *Only One in Three U.S. Households Keeps a Budget*, 2023.
17. Federal Reserve, *Economic Well-Being of U.S. Households Report*, 2023.
18. Charles Schwab, *Modern Wealth Survey*, 2022.
19. Fidelity, *How Much Do I Need to Retire?*, 2023.
20. American Psychological Association, *Stress in America Survey*, 2022.
21. U.S. Bureau of Labor Statistics, *Historical Inflation Data*, 2023.
22. U.S. Bureau of Labor Statistics, *Consumer Price Index Summary*, June 2022.
23. Tax Policy Center, *Average Federal Tax Rates by Income Group*, 2023.

24. Bankrate, *Bank Fees Survey*, 2022.

25. Kiplinger, *The Hidden Costs of Variable Annuities and How to Avoid Them*, 2023

26. FINRA, *National Financial Capability Study*, 2022.

27. Employee Benefit Research Institute, *Automated Savings and Retirement Outcomes*, 2022.

28. Vanguard, *How America Saves*, 2022.

29. Gallup, *Only One in Three Households Keeps a Budget*, 2023.

30. NerdWallet, *2023 Household Credit Card Debt Study*.

31. Federal Reserve, *Consumer Credit – G.19 Report*, 2023.

32. Vanguard, *Average Annual Returns of the S&P 500*, 2023.

33. Fidelity, *The Power of Compounding*, 2022.

34. U.S. Department of Labor, *Saving for Retirement*, 2023.

35. Morningstar, *The Case for Index Funds*, 2022.

36. Schwab, *What Is an ETF?*, 2022.

37. Bankrate, *Financial Security Survey*, 2023.

38. Kaiser Family Foundation, *Medical Debt in the U.S.*, 2022.

39. IRS, *Tax Statistics*, 2023.

40. AARP, *Estate Planning Basics*, 2022.

41. Fidelity, *Pay Yourself First: The Key to Saving*, 2023.

42. Vanguard, *The Power of Automatic Investing*, 2022.

43. U.S. Bank, *Financial Habits Survey*, 2023.

44. Gallup, *Social Influence and Financial Decisions*, 2022.

45. American Psychological Association, *Money and Stress Report*, 2023.

46. Next Gen Personal Finance, *State of Financial Education*, 2023.

47. Pew Research, *Generational Poverty in America*, 2022.

48. Fidelity, *Teaching Kids About Money*, 2023.

49. Vanguard, *How to Think Long-Term with Investments*, 2023.

50. U.S. Bureau of Labor Statistics, *Income and Spending by Age*, 2023.

51. Fidelity, *Decade-by-Decade Retirement Planning Guide*, 2022.

Quick Reference Wealth Terms

401(k) / 403(b)
Employer retirement accounts funded with pre-tax dollars. Often include employer matches.

Active Income
Money earned by working (salary, hourly wages, freelancing). Stops when you stop working.

Assets vs Liabilities
- **Assets:** Things that put money in your pocket (investments, real estate, businesses).
- **Liabilities:** Things that take money out of your pocket (loans, consumer debt).

Bad Debt
Any debt that does not buy an income-producing asset. Credit cards, car loans, and even your primary residence count as bad debt.

Bonds
Loans to companies or governments. Lower risk than stocks, but lower growth.

Cash Flow
Money moving in and out of your life. Positive cash flow means you are saving and investing more than you spend.

Compounding
Money earns money, then that money also earns money. The longer you let it work, the bigger it grows.

Diversification
Spreading investments across different assets to reduce risk.

Estate Planning
Organizing how your wealth transfers after death. Includes wills, trusts, and beneficiary designations.

ETFs (Exchange-Traded Funds)
Bundles of stocks or bonds that trade like a single stock. Low cost, diversified, and beginner-friendly.

Half Rule (Buchholz Method)
A savings and spending system created by Alexis Buchholz. The Half Rule directs you to save at least half of what you earn and live on the other half. It forces discipline, eliminates lifestyle creep, accelerates debt payoff, and creates rapid financial momentum. Even short-term use can permanently reshape spending habits and wealth-building behavior.

HSA (Health Savings Account)
Tax-advantaged account for medical expenses. Contributions, growth, and withdrawals (for health costs) are all tax-free.

Index Funds
ETFs or mutual funds that track an index such as the S&P 500. Simple, cheap, and effective for long-term growth.

Lifestyle Creep
When spending grows as income grows, keeping you stuck in the same spot.

Net Worth
What you own minus what you owe. The single number that shows your financial progress.

Passive Income
Money that continues with little or no effort (dividends, rental income, royalties).

Rebalancing
Adjusting your portfolio back to target allocations by selling some assets and buying others.

Roth IRA
Retirement account funded with after-tax dollars. Grows tax-free and withdrawals in retirement are tax-free.

Stocks
Ownership in a company. Provide growth potential and sometimes dividends.

Umbrella Insurance
Extra liability insurance that adds protection beyond auto and home policies. Inexpensive coverage against lawsuits.

Appendix: Glossary of Key Terms

401(k)
An employer-sponsored retirement account that allows pre-tax contributions. Many employers match part of what you contribute. Withdrawals in retirement are taxed.

403(b)
A retirement plan similar to a 401(k) but offered by schools, nonprofits, and some government organizations.

Active Income
Money you earn by working directly for it, such as a salary, hourly wages, or freelance payments. Active income stops the moment you stop working.

APR (Annual Percentage Rate)
The total yearly cost of borrowing money, including interest and fees. A higher APR means the debt becomes more expensive and grows faster.

Asset Allocation
The process of dividing investments among categories such as stocks, bonds, and cash to balance risk and reward.

Asset Classes
The main categories of investments, such as stocks, bonds, cash, real estate, and alternative assets. Each class behaves differently and serves a different purpose in a portfolio.

Assets
Things you own that have value and can grow or produce income, such as investments, real estate, or businesses.

Automatic Transfers

Scheduled movements of money from your checking account into savings or investments. Automation removes emotion and ensures your system works every month.

Bear Market
A stock market decline of 20 percent or more from recent highs. Often linked to recessions or negative investor sentiment.

Behavioral Finance
The study of how emotions and psychology influence financial decisions. Helps explain overspending, lifestyle creep, and investment mistakes.

Bond
A loan you make to a company or government in exchange for interest payments. Bonds are usually lower risk than stocks but also grow more slowly.

Brokerage Account
An investment account that allows you to buy and sell stocks, ETFs, bonds, and other securities. Unlike retirement accounts, there are no special tax advantages.

Budget
A plan for how you will spend, save, and invest your money each month. A budget gives direction to your cash flow instead of letting it slip away.

Buy Now Pay Later (BNPL)
A modern form of consumer debt that lets you split small purchases into multiple payments. Marketed as harmless, but it conditions you to overspend and creates debt traps.

CAGR (Compound Annual Growth Rate)
The average yearly growth rate of an investment over time. CAGR smooths out ups and downs and shows the true pace of long-term growth.

Capital Gains
The profit from selling an investment at a higher price than you paid. Short-term gains (held less than a year) are taxed at higher rates, while long-term gains (over a year) receive lower tax rates.

Cash Cushion
Extra savings kept aside to cover irregular expenses. A cash cushion protects your budget and prevents overspending.

Cash Flow
The movement of money in and out of your life. Positive cash flow means you are saving and investing more than you spend. Negative cash flow means you are losing ground.

CD (Certificate of Deposit)
A savings product that locks your money for a set period in exchange for a fixed interest rate. Low risk, higher yield than a standard bank account, but the money is tied up until maturity.

Compounding
The process of money earning money, then that new money also earning money. Compounding turns small, consistent contributions into large wealth over time.

Consumer Debt
Debt that does not produce income, such as credit cards, car loans, and personal loans for consumption. Consumer debt drains wealth.

Credit Score
A number that reflects your borrowing history and determines how lenders view you. A high score makes it easier to borrow for income-producing assets, but chasing a credit score just for its own sake is a trap.

Credit Utilization
The percentage of your available credit that you are using. Lower utilization improves your credit score. Experts recommend keeping it below 30 percent.

Debt Avalanche
A debt repayment method where you pay off the highest-interest debt first while making minimum payments on the rest.

Debt Snowball
A debt repayment method where you pay off the smallest balance first for quick wins, then roll those payments into the next debt.

Debt-to-Income Ratio (DTI)
A measure of how much of your monthly income goes toward debt payments. Lenders use DTI to decide whether you can afford a loan.

Diversification
Spreading your investments across different assets, sectors, or regions to reduce risk.

Dividend
A cash payment made to shareholders from company profits. Dividends are a form of passive income.

Dollar-Cost Averaging (DCA)
Investing a fixed amount of money on a regular schedule regardless of market conditions. This smooths out volatility and avoids emotional timing mistakes.

Estate Planning
The process of arranging how your assets will be managed or transferred after death. Tools include wills, trusts, and beneficiary designations.

ETF (Exchange-Traded Fund)
A type of investment fund that trades on an exchange like a stock. ETFs are often low cost, diversified, and simple for beginners.

Emergency Fund
Money set aside for unexpected expenses or lost income. An emergency fund protects you from debt, prevents financial stress, and keeps your long-term investments untouched. Most people aim for

three to six months of living expenses, but any amount of saved cash increases stability.

Generational Poverty
The passing down of poor money habits and limiting beliefs from one generation to the next.

Generational Wealth
The passing down of assets, knowledge, and systems that allow future generations to build on what you created instead of starting from zero.

Half Rule (Buchholz Method)
A savings and spending system created by Alexis Buchholz. The Half Rule directs you to save at least half of what you earn and live on the other half. It forces discipline, eliminates lifestyle creep, accelerates debt payoff, and creates rapid financial momentum. Even short-term use can permanently reshape spending habits and wealth-building behavior.

HSA (Health Savings Account)
A tax-advantaged account used for medical expenses. Contributions are tax-deductible, growth is tax-free, and withdrawals for qualified medical expenses are also tax-free.

High-Yield Savings Account (HYSA)
A savings account that pays a higher interest rate than a regular bank account. Ideal for emergency funds and short-term savings.

Inflation
The rise in prices over time that reduces the purchasing power of money. Inflation silently eats away at cash sitting idle.

Inflation-Adjusted Return
The real return you earn after accounting for inflation. If your investment grows at 6 percent but inflation is 3 percent, your true gain is 3 percent.

Index Fund
A type of mutual fund or ETF that tracks a specific market index, such as the S&P 500. Known for low costs and simplicity.

IRA (Individual Retirement Account)
A personal retirement savings account available in two main forms: Traditional (tax-deductible contributions, taxed withdrawals) and Roth (after-tax contributions, tax-free withdrawals).

Liability
A financial obligation or debt you owe, such as loans, credit cards, or mortgages.

Lifestyle Creep
When your spending rises every time your income increases, keeping you stuck in the same financial position.

Liquidity Trap
A situation where money stays idle because people prioritize safety and hold too much cash instead of investing.

LLC (Limited Liability Company)
A legal structure that separates business assets from personal assets, providing liability protection.

Liquidity
How quickly and easily an asset can be converted into cash without losing value.

Marginal Tax Rate
The tax rate applied to your last dollar of income. Your marginal rate affects decisions about retirement accounts, deductions, and tax planning.

Market Index
A group of stocks that represent a portion of the market, such as the S&P 500 or Dow Jones Industrial Average.

Money Market Account
A bank account that pays higher interest than a traditional savings account. Often comes with limited check-writing. Useful for emergency funds or short-term cash.

Mutual Fund
An investment fund that pools money from many investors to buy a collection of stocks or bonds. Usually more expensive than ETFs.

Net Worth
The difference between what you own (assets) and what you owe (liabilities). Net worth is the scoreboard of financial progress.

P/E Ratio (Price-to-Earnings Ratio)
A measure of a stock's valuation, calculated by dividing the share price by the company's earnings per share.

Passive Income
Income that continues with little or no ongoing effort, such as dividends, rental income, or royalties. Passive income creates freedom.

Portfolio
The collection of all your investments, including stocks, bonds, real estate, and other assets.

Portfolio Diversification
Spreading investments across different assets to lower risk. Diversification prevents a single investment from hurting your entire portfolio.

Principal vs Interest
Principal is the amount you borrow. Interest is the cost you pay to borrow that money. Loans are structured so early payments go mostly toward interest, not principal.

Probate

The legal process where a court decides how your assets are distributed if you die without a proper estate plan. Probate can be slow, costly, and public.

REIT (Real Estate Investment Trust)
A company that owns and operates real estate, paying dividends to shareholders. A way to invest in property without directly owning buildings.

Rebalancing
The process of adjusting a portfolio back to its target asset allocation by selling or buying assets.

Roth IRA
A retirement account funded with after-tax dollars. Money grows tax-free, and withdrawals in retirement are also tax-free.

S&P 500
An index of 500 of the largest U.S. companies, often used as a benchmark for the overall stock market.

Savings Rate
The percentage of your income that you save or invest. A higher savings rate builds wealth faster than higher income ever will. Your savings rate reflects discipline, not salary, and it is the most important number in your financial life.

Stock
Ownership in a company. Stocks provide growth potential and sometimes dividends.

System
A repeatable process that makes money management automatic, such as automatic transfers into savings and investments.

Tax-Advantaged Account

Any financial account that offers tax benefits, such as a 401(k), Roth IRA, Traditional IRA, or HSA. These accounts help your money grow faster by reducing taxes.

Tax Bracket
The income range that determines the rate you pay on your taxable income. Higher income places you in higher tax brackets.

Trust
A legal arrangement where assets are held and managed for beneficiaries. Trusts are often used in estate planning to avoid probate and protect assets.

Umbrella Insurance
An additional layer of liability insurance that covers above and beyond home and auto policies. Provides inexpensive protection against lawsuits.

Volatility
The measure of how much an investment's price fluctuates over time. Higher volatility means higher risk but also higher potential reward.

Will
A legal document that directs how your assets should be distributed after your death. Without a will, the state decides for you.

The Wealth Toolkit

A Companion Resource for *Why You're Still Poor*

This book comes with a full set of downloadable tools to help you put every lesson into practice.

You now understand the systems that build wealth. The next step is putting them into action. To make that process simple, structured, and practical, I created a downloadable **Wealth Toolkit** that includes all the worksheets, planners, and templates referenced throughout this book.

This Wealth Toolkit is free for all readers and available as a downloadable PDF.

Scan the QR code below or visit:

www.bfgwm.com/wealth-toolkit

Inside you'll find tools that help you take control of your money, stay organized, and build wealth with confidence.

Your Wealth Toolkit Includes:

1. **Cash Flow and Savings Systems**
   Budget worksheets, cash-flow templates, and your Half Rule planner.

2. **Debt Elimination Tools**
   Payoff worksheets, credit-building checklist, and planning templates.

3. **Investing and Portfolio Templates**
   Starter allocations, ETF frameworks, and long-term compounding charts.

4. **Net Worth & Progress Trackers**
   Monthly and annual dashboards to measure real growth.

5. **Protection & Risk Management Checklists**
   Insurance, emergency funds, and asset-protection setups.

6. **Room Audit & Network Builder Tools**
   Evaluate your circle, upgrade your rooms, and choose mentors wisely.

7. **Family Wealth Teaching Tools**
   Age-by-age money lessons and generational wealth frameworks.

8. **The 20-Year Wealth Blueprint Template**
   A complete long-term planning system for financial independence and legacy.

These tools are designed to help you build systems, stay consistent, and create results that last. Download your copy and start using them today.

Further Reading & Recommended Resources

Your financial education doesn't end here. If you're ready to keep learning and applying, here are resources that will help you go deeper.

Books by Alexis Buchholz

- **How to Build Portfolios That Actually Work**
  A practical framework for designing investment portfolios that reflect real lives, real income needs, and real tax consequences. This book explains why standardized models fail and works through how to build portfolios around three core goals: growth, income, and after-tax efficiency. Drawing on real client scenarios, it shows how to integrate equities, real estate, thematic investing, and account-level strategy into a flexible, purpose-driven portfolio. Written for investors who want structure, clarity, and results beyond generic allocation charts. ISBN: 979-8-218-77503-2

- **Secrets to Building Wealth**
  A structured playbook for turning income into long-term wealth through disciplined systems and asset ownership. This book lays out a clear progression, starting with cash management and debt control, then moving into stocks, real estate, and business ownership as scalable wealth engines. It emphasizes practical decision rules, real-world tradeoffs, and repeatable strategies for deploying capital, managing risk, and using leverage intelligently as net worth grows. Written for readers who want a clear path forward and the tools to execute it step by step. *Scheduled for release in 2026.*

- **Invest with Precision: The Beginner's Guide to Smart Investing**
  The first book in the *Invest with Precision* series, designed to give new investors a structured, non-gambling approach to investing. This guide explains how markets work, how

different asset classes fit together, and how to build a simple, diversified portfolio using clear rules rather than emotion or speculation. It introduces core concepts like risk, compounding, asset allocation, and basic analysis, while helping readers avoid common beginner mistakes that derail long-term results. Written as a true starting point, it provides the foundation readers need before progressing into more advanced investing and wealth-building strategies. *Scheduled for release in 2026.*

Online Resources

- **BFG Wealth Management Resources**
  Visit www.BFGWM.com for articles, guides, and tools designed to help professionals, entrepreneurs, and families build lasting wealth.

Articles and Insights

- **LinkedIn**
  Follow Alexis on LinkedIn for regular articles, commentary, and practical advice on investing, financial planning, and wealth strategies.

Contact
For speaking, media, or consulting inquiries, reach out to Alexis at **info@bfgwm.com**

About the Author

Alexis Buchholz is the founder and managing partner of BFG Wealth Management, an independent Registered Investment Advisor serving professionals, entrepreneurs, and families across the country. With two decades of experience, Alexis has helped clients cut through financial myths, avoid costly mistakes, and build portfolios that work in the real world.

He is known for his tough-love and practical approach to money. Alexis shows people not just how to invest, but how to think about wealth, create systems that last, and break the cycles that keep families poor. His mission is to make financial literacy and wealth-building accessible to anyone willing to do the work.

Alexis lives in Texas with his wife and four sons, where he continues to invest, write, teach, and advise clients on building wealth that lasts for generations.

Connect
Website: www.bfgwm.com
LinkedIn: linkedin.com/in/alexisbuchholz
Email: info@bfgwm.com

Disclosures

The information in this book is provided for general educational purposes only and is not intended to constitute personalized financial, investment, tax, or legal advice. The concepts, strategies, and examples presented are for illustration only and may not be suitable for all readers. You should consult your own financial advisor, accountant, or attorney before making any financial decisions. Investing involves risk, including possible loss of principal. No investment strategy can guarantee success or protect against loss in declining markets.

Past performance is not indicative of future results. All opinions expressed are those of the author and are subject to change without notice. Any rates of return, growth projections, or compounding examples provided are hypothetical and for educational demonstration only. Actual results vary and cannot be guaranteed. Economic changes, market conditions, interest rates, and individual investor behavior can significantly affect performance.

Tax and legal discussions in this book are general in nature and not specific to any individual situation. You should seek advice from qualified tax or legal professionals regarding your particular circumstances before implementing any strategies discussed. References to insurance, trusts, estate planning, or business entities (such as LLCs or corporations) are provided for informational purposes only. Implementation of such strategies should always be reviewed with licensed professionals and carried out in accordance with applicable state and federal laws.

Case studies and character examples throughout this book are either hypothetical or composites based on real-world experiences. They are not intended to represent any specific client, individual, or actual event. Any resemblance to real persons, living or deceased, is purely coincidental.

Statistics and studies referenced in this book reflect data available at the time of writing. Economic conditions, market performance, inflation levels, and consumer debt trends change over time. Readers are encouraged to consult the latest data and seek professional advice when making financial decisions.

BFG Wealth Management is a Registered Investment Advisor (RIA). Registration does not imply a certain level of skill or training, nor does it imply endorsement by any regulatory authority. Advisory services are offered only to clients and prospective clients in jurisdictions where BFG Wealth Management and its representatives are properly licensed or exempt from licensing.

Reading this book or contacting the author does not create an advisory or fiduciary relationship. Readers should perform their own due diligence and work with licensed professionals before making investment or financial planning decisions.

Legal Notice

The author and publisher make no representations or warranties as to the accuracy, completeness, or timeliness of the information contained herein. The author shall not be liable for any loss or damages, whether direct, indirect, incidental, or consequential, arising from the use of or reliance on this material. Use of this book implies acceptance of these terms.